Ten Years Behind the Mast

The Voyage of Theodora 'R'

By
Fritz Damler

In Memory of R. J. Ward

Other Books by
Fritz Damler

Plunge
Midlife with Snorkel
with Mari Anderson

Suvarov
A Mystery

A Rug to Die For

Okavango
Beware the Ultimate Cure
with John S. Marr M.D.

Thelma and the Whore of Babylon
One Boat – Two Spirits – Big Trouble

Table of Contents

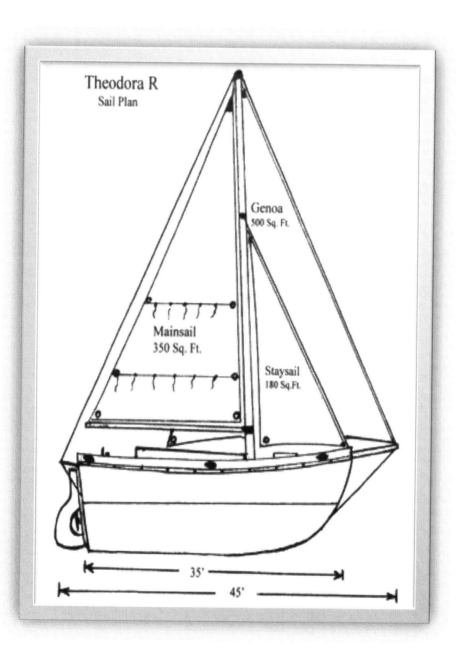

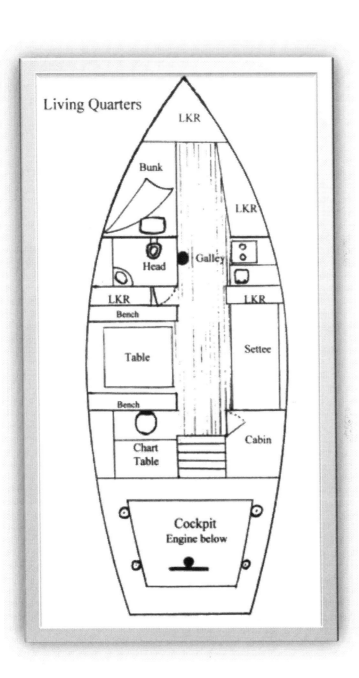

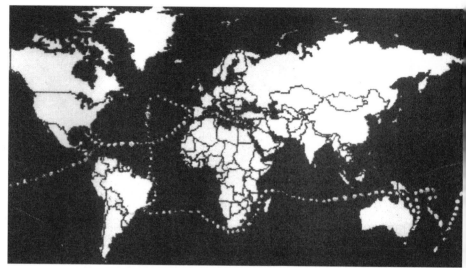

Wake of Theodora R – 1981 - 1991

Introduction

In March of 1992, amidst a boisterous southwest gale, I sailed my 35ft. cutter, THEODORA R, across a ragged Gulf Stream into Lake Worth at West Palm Beach, Florida. I set the anchor just beyond the ship channel near Peanut Island, ran out 150ft. of chain and rode it out for 24 hours. I finally managed to row ashore and contact U.S. Customs from the designated phone. "I'm calling to report my arrival from the Bahamas," I told the officious voice.

"When did you arrive?"

"Yesterday about noon."

"Yesterday?" He exclaimed, "You're required to report in on arrival!'"

"Well, yeah, I know that, but it was blowing 40 knots. I couldn't leave the boat."

"Don't you have a cell phone?"

What the devil is a cell phone, I thought. "Uh, no."

Deep sigh. "Okay, point of departure?"

"West Palm."

"Date?"

"February 22, 1982."

Long silence. "Ten years ago?"

"Correct."

Short chuckle. "Oh boy, they're gonna love this one."

The Bahamas, of course, had been my last port of call, but in the previous ten years I'd racked up several hundred ports of call around the world. I'm still baffled by the logistics of how it all started and in retrospect realize I'd taken it one day at a time.

In 1974 I was invited to join a delivery crew contracted to sail a 41ft. Morgan sloop from Ft. Lauderdale, Florida to San Carlos Bay, on the west coast of Mexico. The trip lasted 5 months and covered 5000 miles from the Caribbean through the Panama Canal and up the west coat of Central America.

1

It was this trip that showed me what traveling via cruising sailboat was all about and introduced me to the basics of sailing and navigation. What I didn't realize at the time was how easy I'd had it being the crew. I was totally oblivious to the responsibility that lies with the skipper and wouldn't come to understand this until I was at the helm of my own vessel. But hey, that was years down the road and the travel bug had bitten me big time. I yearned to see the rest of the world, experience things first hand instead of second and third hand from books or the media. There didn't seem to be much to the sailing part of things, just raise the sails and off you go.

At the time, I had my own business building guitars near Albuquerque, New Mexico. With a complete woodshop at my disposal and being naturally handy with tools and such, I decided to build my own boat. I planned to spend 6 or 7 years building the boat with spare time and money so when completed I could place the business on ice and lease out the house for the cruising kitty. Someone once said that life seems to get in the way of the best-laid plans. Dang if they weren't right.

Marriage didn't appear to complicate the issue. I'd met Linda at the ambulance service where she and I worked nights as paramedics, she for a living and me more for fun. The idea of sailing around the world at some later date didn't faze her. I began work in earnest on a 36-foot center cockpit Brewer design, learning from books as the piles of wood chips grew. Three years and $3000 later I was planking the hull of what could only be a big sailboat in my backyard and I had to admit it was quite impressive. All the major structural components were oak, mahogany and fir, laminated with a special epoxy adhesive that sadly, in the spring of 1978, broke down completely. The vessel was rendered useless in the nautical sense, but made for a terrific sauna and a substantial pile of firewood – I was devastated. Not so, my wife. I believe now that was a look of relief in her eyes.

My lack of enthusiasm for starting over combined with my ever-growing urge to travel the world forced plan B. Simply stated this was to sell the house to buy the boat and sell the business to pay for the sailing. The catch here of course was that there would be nothing to return to - an unpopular decision with my wife. But I reasoned that a lot could happen in 10 years so let's worry about it then. I still find that a pretty convincing argument.

Selling a sole proprietorship craft business was not easy, but combined with a two-year apprenticeship, I eventually found a willing buyer. I thought the house would be easy to sell, but when the time came in 1980, interest rates had begun a slow relentless climb. This nasty trick of the Federal Reserve Bank caused three potential buyers to fail loan qualifications before closing papers could be signed. Frustrated, Linda and I took a trip down the East Coast looking for "The" boat. For me this would have to be a wooden vessel for two reasons: 1- my natural affinity towards woodworking and 2- the organic nature of the substance in regards to nourishing the soul. Like the difference between a log cabin and a mobile home. One may argue that interior joinery would make up for that, but I can honestly say from first hand experience, the vibes are totally different.

Unfortunately for us we actually found the Theodora R late in the trip tied to a dock in Ft. Lauderdale. I knew the moment I stepped aboard, and the boat didn't so much as flinch, Theodora R was a serious contender. Built in 1936 of pitchpine on double-sawn oak frames she had 35 feet of wide fir decks, spruce mast and rakish bowsprit that extended her sail plan to 45 feet. Rats, I had really hoped this wouldn't happen. As an added kick in the teeth, interest rates shot past 15% and any hope of selling the house vanished and kept my dream out of reach.

Some months went by and the Theodora R was still for sale, giving the owner and me the incentive to come up with variation A on alternate plan B. I offered to trade the equity in the house straight across for the boat and find a third party to buy the house on a personal real estate contract, the papers to be held by the boat owner. In other words, a real estate trade. It took 6 months, 2 lawyers, 6 million phone calls and a ream of paper, but ultimately, the deal was done. So began a 10-year circumnavigation.

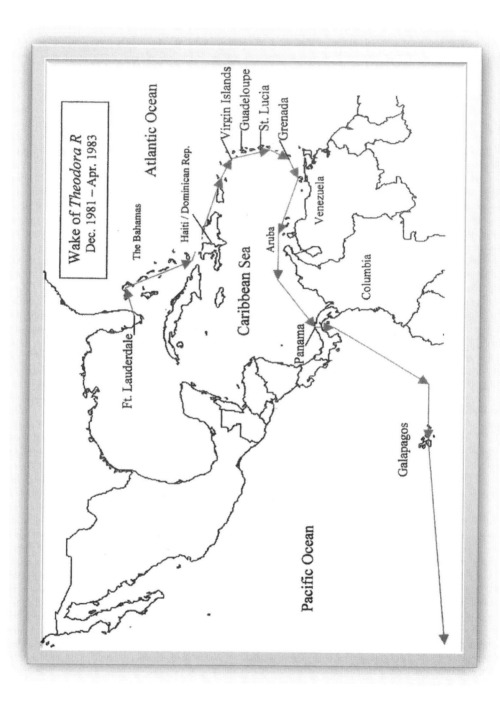

Wake of *Theodora R*
Dec. 1981 – Apr. 1983

Atlantic Ocean

Virgin Islands
Guadeloupe
St. Lucia
Grenada

The Bahamas

Haiti / Dominican Rep.

Caribbean Sea

Venezuela

Aruba

Columbia

Ft. Lauderdale

Panama

Galapagos

Pacific Ocean

Fritz Damler

Busting out of Madagascar

The First Quarter Mile

"If this wind holds we'll be there in..."

I had just turned 32 when I signed over the house and piled all our worldly goods into and on top of an old Volvo sedan. We drove out of Albuquerque in a blizzard and followed that cold front all the way to Florida, arriving in Ft. Lauderdale at 3 a.m. on a mid December morning in 1981. There was a film of ice on the mud puddles.

For two months, Summerfield boat yard, up the New River in Ft. Lauderdale, would be our first home aboard the Theodora R. There existed that warm camaraderie of the cruising set, of shared meals, free advice and never-ending discussions of marine toilets - a comfortable routine destined for change.

It came as a shock when the last pre-cruise chore was crossed off the list that for the first month had never diminished but had grown to a staggering length. Not so much a shock that we could leave, but a shock that we had to leave. Pulling up roots in Albuquerque, my home for fifteen years, had been a welcome task compared to the thought of actually putting to sea. Here it was, the big dream come true and I balked. Conferring with Linda, I found she had more trouble with the move from New Mexico than the idea of setting sail. That's when the captain versus crew thing finally hit me. The captain is ultimately responsible for everything aboard the vessel and now it wouldn't be just talk. The coiled snake in my guts raised its ugly head and smiled. I was damn nervous.

To our credit, we slipped TR's moorings like old salts early one morning in mid February 1982 and headed down river. Once underway, with the smooth thrum of TR's diesel bucking a rising tide and safely negotiating our first opening bridge, the snake resumed hibernation. For the next ten years, every time I left harbor the reptile would slither around for the first quarter mile, a little reminder that I best pay attention and that no one out here but Mother Nature makes the rules.

We dropped the hook around noon at the last remaining free anchorage along the Ft. Lauderdale portion of the intercoastal waterway. Summerfield's and TR had put a mighty strain on our budget and it was a relief to stop the hemorrhage of cash for the time being and let our reserves build. Between the sale of my business and a piece of real estate I had invested in, we had $450 per month coming in for the next ten years. I figured if we were prudent and stayed out of harm's way, the money would be enough to see us through. Linda wasn't comfortable about not contributing financially, which I admitted I could understand, but I said if it would make her feel better, the next ten years could be on her. That helped some but not entirely. I was still in denial about her level of desire concerning this adventure.

Among the flood of free advice sloshing about the boat yard was the practical tip that if you left Florida at 10 P.M. you'd make a daylight arrival on the shallow Bahama Banks. We tuned in to NOAA weather radio for the evening forecast, which called for a southeasterly shift in the 15-knot winds that generally blow from the northeast. Due to warnings about drug trafficking around the southern Bahamian island of Andros, our plan was to head for the Abacos in the northern Bahamas, what looked like an easy northeast run across the Gulf Stream from Port Everglades. With a favorable forecast, we stowed our remaining stores and secured anything that looked like it might come adrift. Long before the anchor came up, the snake had flexed its coils and had me pacing the deck. There would definitely be no problem staying awake for the overnighter. Traffic on the waterway was light and we hoisted sail in the turning basin before clearing the breakwater. The wind, as promised, had shifted towards the south. As soon as we passed the last buoy marking the spoil area north of the harbor channel we fell off to a nice reach and laid our course. For the first hour we smoked along at 6 knots under full main and working jib. The stars shown like halogen lamps as we left the brown haze of Florida behind and the wind had that clean fresh taste, one that seemed to holler, "Yeah! It's okay to breathe this stuff." My grin put those stars to shame.

Linda thought it was pretty cool too. She took the helm and I went below to plot our progress. In short order I popped up the companionway and said those fateful words, "If this wind holds, we'll be there in...". I'm not superstitious but I don't whistle in a breeze and these days I rarely put to words any phrase that implies consistency in the wind. By midnight the wind had backed into the east and TR tried valiantly to shoulder aside the six-foot square seas. Each time she'd get up a head of speed, her bow would plunge into the face of one of those suckers and she'd stop dead. Her constitution was strong but the hull design being what it was, full well forward with a bluff entry, she would only tack through 120 degrees on a good day. We bashed around for another hour and I could hear water sloshing in the bilge, an indication that the garboards were working when we beat hard to weather. This is typical of older wood boats and means there is movement around the mast step during periods of stress. I would tolerate this for three years before the Indian Ocean made TR cry for mercy. Several of the lockers had sprung open and spewed dishes, canned goods and who-knows-what all over the cabin. It made a hell of a racket. I flipped on the bilge pump. Score 1 for the Gulf Stream. As soon as we turned around a tangible peace settled over TR – Mother Nature giving us a pat on the head.

Streetlights along the beach at Ft, Lauderdale still looked a couple miles off in the pre-dawn mist. In my now diminished state of awareness I thought we were well outside the outer channel marker when we blundered into the spoil area. TR bounced off the bottom three times striking hard once before she answered the helm and tacked out of danger. A vivid image of boat wreckage awash on the beach flashed in my mind. I swear I heard a toilet flush, but that was just my pancreas dumping pure adrenaline into my system. I kept a sharp ear tuned to the sound of the bilge pump sucking air – a very sweet sound – as we sailed past the breakwater.

Motoring back to our anchorage, I noticed the heat gauge pegged in the red. I shut down the diesel and being hearty sailors we attempted to hoist the sails but the halyard jammed in the lower shrouds. Before the SOB came free we drifted onto a muddy shoal and stuck fast. Some wise-guy in a speedboat cruised past and yelled, "Shallow over there, skip." Nothing like a little salt in the gaping wound of my ego. By the time we cleared the halyard, the engine temp had dropped a bit so I fired her up momentarily and we backed off the shoal and began to tack up the waterway. At the last sharp bend I spun the wheel hard to port and the chain jumped off the helm sprocket. Rudderless, TR plowed into another mud-bank. At this point all we could do was laugh. I kicked the anchor overboard and took down the sails − coffee time. Fortunately, the tide was on the rise and by the time I tightened the belt on the cooling pump and we had relaxed with a mug of brew, TR was afloat.

I dove for an inspection at the anchorage and was relieved to find only a dent in the lead keel where she'd struck hard. The damage, it turned out, wasn't to the boat, but to all my power tools. They'd been soaked in bilge water. I had hoped for a good day's rest but spent the day at the public fountain, dismantling and rinsing off the salt with the hope they would survive to run another day. The tedious chore gave me time to reflect on the past twelve hours: almost lost the boat due to a navigational error, ran aground twice, trashed my power tools, butchered my ego, and undermined the crew's confidence in the skipper − not bad for the first day out. Linda's attitude took a more positive bent. She thought it was great that we got all the bad stuff out of the way right from the get-go.

Two days later, with another "favorable" forecast and the snake doing the boogaloo, TR once again nosed into the Gulf Stream. This time the wind waited a little longer before forcing us back, making West Palm Beach our new port of refuge. Five days of fortified trade winds kept us harbor-bound, giving us time to discover the motor for the generator had no compression, the shaft in the outboard had stripped its splines and the old Loran navigation system had a fatal flaw. Once we'd cleared all that junk off the boat, the extra space prompted us to fabricate a bulky wire fish trap, another one of those gems from the free advice pool. This would supposedly guarantee an endless supply of fresh fish throughout the cruise. Now, if only the wind would cooperate. I kept telling myself we had plenty of time and the odd setback could always be turned to our advantage if we let it.

A weak cold front finally clocked the wind into the southwest and we broke for the Bahamas. Ten miles out the wind died completely. We decided it was time to let the iron genny show us her stuff and motored calmly across the Gulf Stream. We arrived on the Banks at daybreak as planned but the fog was so thick it made no difference. I tuned in one faint radio signal for a general line of position and the depth sounder showed 12 feet of water.

The clear path across the northern banks is marked by Riding Rock Light, the light in this case being noted on the chart as not working. I told Linda I thought we were close but a wee bit south. No one was more surprised than I was, when Riding Rock loomed out of the fog two minutes after we turned north. Of course I kept that to myself since after my last great assumption I felt it necessary to shore up the crew's confidence.

Baggywrinkles prevent chafe

The Thorny Path East

"Safety Inspection? Are you guys nuts!?"

The Bahamas are only fifty miles from Florida, but it truly is another world and the ultimate cruiser's playground. Linda finally got to experience first hand everything I'd been telling her about for years. Our wind filled in gently from the north and TR glided silently across the banks on flat seas. As the sun rose, lotion replaced clothes and we took turns perched on the bowsprit watching the seabed scroll by. Even whipping up a hearty breakfast was a pleasure.

Our first foreign landfall hove into sight in the late afternoon, a small crescent shaped cay with a wispy fringe of casuarinas and coconut palms. We had the place to ourselves, which proved to be the norm throughout our Bahamian cruise. Once the hook was down and we were secure in our little piece of paradise, a toast seemed to be in order. Beer in the Bahamas was rumored to be expensive so we had laid in a couple of cases to defray costs. After two months in the boatyard, noticing that anyone with a fridge aboard was either working on it or had already condemned it to an icebox, we decided to forego refrigeration. Bilge-cool was okay by us and that's where we'd stacked the 48 aluminum cans. When I reached into the bilge, the cans seemed suspiciously light. As I removed them one by one, flat stale beer oozed from the chalky surface of the cans. On close inspection we found them to be riddled with tiny pinholes from saltwater corrosion – another casualty from our first attempted crossing when the bilge was awash. From now on there would only be glass bottles in the bilge. Fortunately there was a bottle of Bacardi aboard and the toast commenced with a tall rum punch.

We cleared in at Green Turtle Cay, our first exposure to the local inhabitants, their culture and bureaucracy. The fact that the customs office was closed at 2 P.M. and I had to walk around town to find the person in charge was a pretty good indication about how informal things were (remember, this is 1982). The Bahamas had only achieved independence in 1975, so there was a strong wave of nationalism in the country. Lucky for us we'd sewn together a new Bahamian flag, which hung from our starboard flag halyard, otherwise it would have been a $50 fine.

We poked around the Abacos for a few weeks and unless one is intimately acquainted with the Bahama Banks, prudent movement is limited to daylight hours using what is known as eyeball navigation. This is a takeoff on paint by number called steer by color. To my knowledge there is no better place to learn this invaluable technique than the Bahamas and I'll be forever grateful for the two months we spent in those crystal waters learning the subtle nuances between cloud shadow and grass or scoured hard bottom and sand. But the most instructive aspect of sailing in such clear water was being able to actually see the submerged obstacles that created variations in surface ripples. In poor light or murky water, those ripples are the only indication of what danger lurks below.

The relatively calm waters also allowed us to experiment with TR's best points of sail and mess with the wind-vane steering system that we named Bill. Bill had what is called a servo-pendulum rudder, a long spruce paddle that hung in the water and connected through simple linkage to a wind vane mounted on the stern. Once on course, the vane was set vertical to the wind. When the vessel wanders off course the wind vane is blown to one side, turning the paddle, which is then forced by the water to port or starboard. The paddle is attached to a quadrant from which lines are run to a hub on the wheel. As the paddle swings, the wheel is turned, and hence the rudder, to bring the vessel back on course. It took me a good year to figure out that the sails must be well balanced and the boat holding course on her own before Bill would do a proper job. Prior to that, Bill was a constant source of frustration and, I'm embarrassed to say, severely tongue-lashed for insubordination – sorry Bill. Once Bill and I reached an understanding, there was never a finer member of the crew.

In a small bay on the south edge of the Abacos, we were introduced to conch. I had noticed a local fisherman diving nearby and tossing large shells into his skiff. When he towed the lot to shore and started the cleaning process, I swam in and asked him what he was doing. He asked me how long I'd been in the Bahamas and I told him a month. He gave me an odd look and said, "You been in the Bahamas a month and you don't know nothin' bout conch?"

I shook my head.

He pointed to a spot next to him, "Sit here. I'm gonna show you what you missin'."

And that is how I learned about harvesting, cleaning and preparing conch. Conch meat is similar to most other shellfish, octopus and lobster, so the lesson translated well when the conch beds were left oceans behind. He also told me to use the conch guts to bait the fish trap, which until now had been just getting in the way.

The mouth of the trap narrowed down to about 6 inches, limiting the size of whatever swam in, or so we thought. I swear grouper are shape-shifters. The first time we hauled the trap, a monster Nassau grouper was flailing around inside. He weighed in at about twenty pounds. How he got in through that small opening was a mystery, extraction a challenge. The access door was clearly inadequate and we finally had to wait until he expired in the trap and rework the door before he could be considered supper. Between diving for conch, spearing lobster and catching grouper in the trap, we indeed feasted on the bounty of the sea.

The big picture was to spend the first year in the Caribbean as a shakedown cruise and reevaluate the situation before crossing Panama. Had I known what would shake out in the shakedown, I'd probably have done things differently.

Our shakedown list was a mile long and each day we tried to cross off at least one item. It was all stuff that didn't need to be done in a boatyard. Hence this common definition of cruising: doing boat maintenance in foreign and exotic places. It didn't take us long to realize that one item per day was overly ambitious, especially if we were to do any sailing. The list got reshuffled periodically based on the current level of priority. Sometimes there were unplanned surprises requiring our immediate attention. The first of those came while anchored at Little San Salvador, a classic deserted island sitting in the middle of the Bahama chain. After two quiet days of diving and whipping the ends on all our rigging line, a front moved through, shifting the prevailing east wind to the north. I decided it would be a good time to jump off for the Virgin Islands, since we'd be able to sail due east with the favorable wind. When I turned the key, there was no response from the starter. A few minutes of troubleshooting pointed to a serous problem with TR's starter motor. We weren't far from Nassau. If I couldn't fix the problem, we could sail the eighty or so miles to get it repaired. Thus began two days of remove and install exercises. The inside solder joint on one of the heavy copper terminals had fractured. The only thing I had on board for this sort of repair was a propane torch with a flame that jeopardized all the windings in the motor. Creative use of some asbestos strips eventually solved that problem but it took six attempts before the starter was successfully resuscitated. I felt pretty good about handling the repair on my own. It also went a long way to convincing Linda that we'd be okay cruising the boonies.

By then, of course, the wind had clocked into the east again. (Do you see a pattern here?) We set our sights on Clarencetown, halfway down the Atlantic side of Long Island, a place I remembered fondly from the boat delivery in 1974. We set sail in the morning and that night we were punching into Atlantic swells off the north end of Long Island. At 10 P.M., I told Linda I was going to shorten sail. The words had just cleared my mouth when TR threw a wall of green water into the genoa. There was a tremendous POP when a seam blew out. Chaos reigned as TR slewed broadside to the seas and we tried to subdue the madly flapping sail. In the mayhem one of the sheet lines wrapped itself around the prop and jammed in the rudder. How it happened, I haven't a clue, but there it was. We dropped the mainsail and hoisted the staysail, which forced TR's bow downwind. I tethered myself to one of the winches and slid into chilly water. I wasn't too keen on going over the side in those seas. Fortunately we had an underwater light so I didn't have to assess the problem by feel. The wrap on the prop wasn't a problem but where the line had wedged between the hull and rudder was a bitch to pull free, especially with the stern rising and falling in six-foot throws. It seemed the prop was intent on decapitation. With Linda working the wheel and me jerking the line, we finally won the round. I decided the new rule would be that after an experience like that we qualified for three days without boat maintenance. In this case we had the damaged sail to consider, but hey, we had a spare.

The 12-mile light on Long Island guided us in to a safe cove on the leeward side. Without that light I'd have never attempted a night approach due to off-lying reefs. We spent two idyllic days recuperating and then the weather forecast assured us of another cold front working its way through the Bahamas. This could be our sleigh-ride to the Virgin Islands. Early the third morning we could see the front, a long, dark cigar-shaped cloud closing from the northwest. The wind behind these fronts typically blows 20 to 25 knots. After donning our foul weather gear, we double-reefed the main and set the staysail, before motoring around the headland. The cloud was directly overhead when a strong gust filled TR's sails and she surged forward for about 15 seconds. Then all was quiet. We waited... and waited.... But that was it, one puff. It was beginning to look like a short blue-water run to the Virgin Islands wasn't meant to be. A quick peek at the chart made Rum Cay, thirty miles east, the logical next landfall.

The ocean soon glassed over as we motored towards Rum, but as the day wore on, a heavy groundswell rolled in and TR labored up and over the ten-foot hills. First I noticed the smell, that distinctive hot engine smell. I looked and again the gauge was in the red. No sweat, I thought, just tighten the belt and we'd be good to go. But no, there wasn't any adjustment left on the pump bracket. This required removing the pump and drilling new holes in the bracket. Under normal conditions this would pose no problem, but TR now wallowed in the big rollers rolling on her beam-ends. There was nothing to be done about it. If we raised a sail it would be rags in no time. Linda held on to all the loose bits and pieces while the drill bits and I rolled around in the hot, smelly engine room. This was a supreme test for seasickness and we both passed with exceptional marks. An hour later we were under way, but had lost valuable daylight. The cruising guide said there was a

5-mile light at the head of the bay where the main settlement was. This was encouraging, but as we rounded the western end of Rum and turned into the bight we couldn't make out anything but a small cluster of lights several miles off where I assumed the village was. The bight is protected by a barrier reef but the reef only extends part way, making it necessary to enter at least a mile for any protection. With the groundswell running we would have to go a bit further. There are scattered coral heads and a couple of shoal areas in the bight so we lowered the anchor six feet and moved forward at 1 knot. I used the cluster of lights as a bearing to avoid the shoals and held our breath. Almost an hour later I watched in dismay as the cluster of lights suddenly changed aspect and moved to the south, the green navigation light of a good size ship clearly visible −YIKES! To hell with rolly conditions, we dropped anchor. The next morning found TR sitting calmly over a wide circle of white sand surrounded by dark brown coral. We definitely used up a lot of good anchoring karma on that one.

The lights, I discovered, had been the mailboat offloading cargo then heading back to Nassau. And that 5-mile navigation light? A small kerosene lantern set atop a post with enough fuel to last 3 hours. Visible range was about 300 yards and that was when the fronds of a nearby palm tree didn't obscure the feeble glow entirely.

The trip to Rum qualified us for another three-day break from boat work. We hauled out our scuba gear and, on the recommendation from the local dive resort, spent a day exploring the outer reef. Linda and I had taken a PADI dive course in Albuquerque. For our open water dive we'd driven 2 hours east to Santa Rosa, home of the famed blue hole: fifty feet across and a hundred feet deep. The blue hole was perfectly clear for the first dive. If you were lucky you might spot the odd tadpole, but visibility decreased with each subsequent dive as the muck on the bottom was stirred up. A hundred feet down, a metal grate covered the entrance to a narrow, descending tunnel that was the water source. The grate was installed after a couple of divers drowned, then had to be retrieved, from the 250-foot mark. No one knows the depth of that tunnel. For us novices, the blue hole seemed a truly awesome dive.

The barrier reef at Rum Cay extends for miles and has a steep drop off on the Atlantic side with an outstanding wall of coral. Creatures abound from delicate fluorescent fish to 30 pound grouper and the odd lobster. The blue hole had been our last dive, so you can imagine how blown away we were amidst the colorful abundance of coral and sea life. We made two dives that day, neither deeper than 60 feet, but that was plenty. I've since found most everything worth seeing usually lies in less than 30 feet of water. To refill the tanks, we had our own compressor aboard, a mix of parts I'd found at the flea market and assembled in Florida. The unit was fairly small and took 45 minutes to fill a standard 72 cubic foot tank. That equates to a lot of racket in an otherwise quiet setting and I believe it to be the reason we didn't use our scuba gear often.

Late that afternoon, I heard the familiar rattle of anchor chain running out. It seemed fairly close, so I hopped on deck via the forward hatch to have a look. As I've mentioned, the anchorage at Rum is spacious, probably close to a square mile in size, making it hard for me to fathom why anyone would anchor so close given TR was the only other boat there. I watched the guy set his anchor and even returned his friendly, yet clueless wave. Once he'd shut the motor down, his 45-foot ketch settled in about 30 feet off our port bow. An Eagles tune, Hotel California, drifted across the space. If the wind shifted, the big American flag on the stern would polish TR's forestay. In crowded conditions his proximity was acceptable, but out here? That's when Linda told me we still had one scuba tank to fill. Ten minutes after I started the compressor, the guy was on his foredeck, the electric windlass cranking in the chain. He and his wife dinghied over later and we invited them aboard for sundowners. During the course of a very pleasant evening that ended with dinner aboard their boat (they had caught a ten-pound tuna on the way in) Jim admitted to anchoring too close at first but the compressor had really convinced him. Over the next ten years, I would often experience this phenomenon of one boat attracting others. I found that for some it was an urge to be social, others figured you must have scoped out the anchorage and found the best spot, or in Jim's case, curiosity about an old wood boat. The latter would usually tickle my vain streak and, if asked, I'd gush on about TR until their eyes glazed over. I like my privacy, and if sharing an anchorage will always try and keep a respectable distance from another vessel. For privacy reasons I also shun marinas unless I have dire need of the facility.

We chose a perfect tradewind day for the jaunt to Clarencetown, a 6-hour reach capped by grilled grouper on the beach. But here we had to make a decision, wait for another front and hope it would carry us all the way to the Virgin Islands, or take the Thorny Path east. Thorny because it would require coastal hopping along Hispanola and Puerto Rico, using the offshore winds at night to make our easting. A high-pressure ridge sat over the Bahamas funneling in strong easterlies, so after two days we chose the Thorny Path and headed for Great Inagua at the bottom of the Bahama chain. We set the hook after a brisk 24-hour sail. The lee side of Great Inagua provided a fairly calm anchorage, encouraging us to stay a day or two. I hitched a ride to the Morton Salt facility with the idea of procuring a spare belt for TR's cooling pump. I was amazed at the extent of their spares warehouse and came away with two spare belts for a fair price. I had just returned victorious when a fluke in the weather shifted the wind into the north. After the all-nighter we were bushed, but the north wind was too much to pass up. Plus, it made for an uncomfortable anchorage. We hoisted sail and laid our course east.

Our wind held through the night, but at dawn, clocked into the northeast. Haiti lay ten miles south, now a dark purple lump on the horizon that looked like a sleeping dinosaur. In two hours we'd be off the entrance to Cap Haitian, a well-protected harbor and good place to wait out the daytime easterlies. The only catch was, it was Haiti, which was rumored to be in political strife. We weren't sure about putting in and deferred our decision to the last possible moment. About an hour later, TR tossed another bow wave into the spare genoa with the same destructive results as the last time – another good point in favor of Cap Haitian. As we neared the harbor entrance we spotted another American flagged sailboat motoring in circles a mile offshore. I hailed them on the radio and they said they were waiting another hour before entering to avoid overtime charges, which they had heard to be unreasonable. Linda and I were glad of the company and despite our fatigue, decided it might be wise to wait another hour as well.

As it turned out, the port captain charged us overtime anyway because he'd seen us from his house and left early so he'd be in the office when we arrived. We had to cough up an extra five bucks on top of the ten-dollar cruising permit.

Haiti would leave an indelible imprint on my soul. I had traveled extensively in the U.S. and Mexico, had seen the city slums, the barrios, the rural South, but it didn't prepare me for Haiti. Now this was POOR. In relative terms, we were now the ultra-rich. A chain-link fence kept unauthorized people out of the commercial harbor where we had been advised to lay alongside an unfinished concrete quay. Beyond the fence, a desperate press of humanity waited with their hands out. One clever boy, Peter, talked his way past the guard and offered his services as guide and gopher for $10 a day. The four of us hired him on the spot, especially after having run the gauntlet through town on an earlier sightseeing mission. We asked him how he came to speak English so well. He said, "Without English, you starve."

A series of conical, 7000 Ft. peaks surrounded Cap Haitian. Through the mist, one of them appears to be wearing a small square hat. This was the Citadel; a fort built by one of Napoleon's generals, and said to be the 8th wonder of the world. A brutal tyrant, Christof, built the Citadel with the blood of a thousand slaves to protect himself from his boss. Our newfound friend was adamant that we not miss the Citadel, the hottest tourist attraction around.

We took a taxi to the base of the mountain, where against our better judgement, we agreed to rent ponies for the seven-mile climb to the top. This also meant we had to hire a boy with a willow switch for each pony in order to keep the pathetic creatures moving. When presented with our mounts, undernourished, rickets-riddled scraps of horseflesh, we couldn't bring ourselves to ride the poor beasts so we paid off the whipping boys and led the ponies up the mountain. Peter thought we were nuts.

What had looked like a small structure from the harbor, was an immense concrete and stone fortress, the likes I'd never dreamed possible to build. Designed for thousands to withstand the long siege, a complex water catchment fed a subterranean cistern that in itself was a feat of engineering. Unmounted cannons and stacks of softball-size cannonballs were scattered like so much yard-art throughout. Since only a halfhearted attempt was being made to run the place as an organized tourist attraction, we were left on our own to explore at will. I came away knowing I'd never really have to see another fort. We'd seen the ultimate.

That night, someone came along side and cut loose one of TR's sheet lines. Foolishly I had left them laid out instead of coiled and stored. I mentioned it to Peter while Linda and I repaired our two torn genoas on the quay. Later that day he took me to see the police. A sergeant in a crisp blue uniform explained through Peter that he could get my rope back, but I would have to witness the punishment. I asked Peter what sort of punishment. He told me the man would be beaten with sticks. I bid the sergeant good day and told him whoever had the rope was welcome to it. I was ready to leave Haiti.

It hadn't taken long to realize we'd be broke in no time handing out money to every needy hand. To this day I still don't give money away on the street, but do give away food or clothing if I have it to give. Linda and Sarah raided their respective stores lockers and when we left, Peter was a nutritionally wealthy man.

I was depressed and confused by Haiti. How could this deprivation exist so close to the land of plenty? It would take a couple of years traveling before I understood that my country's political and economic agenda wasn't about doing the right thing in terms of a general world view. I knew it could screw up big time as pointed out by the Vietnam fiasco, but I was naive, and pretty much in denial about America's shady side.

The offshore breeze usually kicked in around 10 p.m., enabling us to motorsail due east until ten the next morning. Our next stop would be Puerto Plata in the Dominican Republic, a huge step up from Haiti. The most memorable aspect of the visit was our first attempt at anchoring stern-to to the jetty. I rounded up and Linda let loose the anchor, paying out chain as we backed into a tight space like old salts. Everything seemed to go all right except the chain wouldn't come taut. It turns out that the trip line on the anchor had caught in the bobstay and the anchor was hanging just below the surface of the muddy water. I decided to row out the anchor, piling 70-feet of muddy chain into the stern of the dinghy. I got out about twenty feet when the chain started to run out faster and faster over the stern. Mud flew off the links covering me from the crotch up. I had to avert my face just to breathe. When all the chain had run out and I'd tossed over the anchor, the guy on the boat next to us said, "There are people who dream all their lives about doing this."

It took three more thorny night passages to reach Samana, at the east end of the Dominican Republic. We rested a few days and took one long walk into the surrounding countryside. Linda had befriended a young girl and she acted as our guide, introducing us to all her relatives living in the hills. Her parent's house, a sturdy plywood shack with thatched roofing, was about two miles from town. Her mother offered us a drink of water and when she handed us the cups, we were surprised to find ice in them. The ice block had been carried from town and stored in a cooler. We felt like royalty. I was also intrigued to see her baby brother, a mere toddler, playing in the dirt with a 24-inch machete. This didn't concern his mother in the least. I guess it makes sense to get them started young, because living in the bush, that machete would soon be a permanent extension of his arm.

We took advantage of two days of dead calm to motor all the way to San Juan. It seemed we were back in Florida – all the mod cons, easy phone calls to the states, and more people speaking English than in Miami. But anchored nearby was Sea Witch, another wood boat, somewhat younger and daintier than TR but with a proud, jutting bowsprit. She had just completed a circumnavigation and the owners were kind enough to relate their adventures and field endless questions from all us wannabes. Those cockpit sessions reaffirmed my decision to see the world and I'd return to TR more excited than ever. Not so Linda, who was already homesick and looked upon the planned voyage as "A ten year prison sentence."

Clearly she was not taking well to the cruising life. The division of labor was a prime issue. She wasn't housewife material and had enjoyed a professional career as an emergency paramedic. With me being mechanically minded and the general handyman, the bulk of the domestic chores fell to her i.e.: cooking, cleaning and shopping. She didn't show much interest in navigation and I wasn't about to shove it down her throat. She was along for the ride, but her true interests lay elsewhere. We had lots of company coming to join us in the Virgin Islands and I had my fingers crossed that being able to share her experience with friends and family would maybe turn on a few green lights.

We left San Juan late one night to catch the offshore breeze. A huge groundswell was running and it took all my concentration to keep the bow into the rollers. A quarter mile out, over the sound of TR's diesel, I began hearing an odd buzz from astern. Linda noticed it too and after a quick look told me there were four guys dressed in dark clothes in an inflatable dinghy with no lights directly behind us. My first thought was drug runners. I chanced a look over my shoulder and saw the flash of a penlight across TR's stern. Oh, Shit! I glanced around the cockpit searching for a possible weapon. My eyes settled on the bronze winch handle. The next thing I heard, was the outboard accelerating. The dinghy came along our port side and a guy yelled, "We're the U.S. Coast Guard and we're coming aboard."

I was skeptical to say the least. Since when did they come aboard uninvited? The sea conditions were dicey to begin with and anybody could say they were the Coast Guard. The next thing we knew two burly men jumped aboard and scrambled into the cockpit. One pulled out a clipboard and told us they were there to do a safety inspection. I couldn't believe my ears. "A safety inspection? Are you guys nuts? We've been in the harbor for five days, why didn't you do it then?"

"Doesn't matter," the guy said, " We're doing it now."

I had to wonder if the officer in charge of public relations for the Coast Guard knew these guys were out here acting like Gestapo. As I struggled with the helm, Linda showed them our flares, fire extinguishers and flotation devices. The scene was totally surreal. When they had finished, I told them they were lucky to be alive.

"What do you mean?" The clipboard asked.

I told them my thoughts when we first noticed them and explained that there were cruisers out here who would have gladly turned them into shark bait with a shotgun for attempting a stealth approach at night. I think my words fell on deaf ears.

Shortly after dawn, a giant cruise liner out of San Juan passed nearby. From its stern spewed thousands of plastic plates, cups, utensils and other assorted crap. We sailed through this garbage slick for close to an hour. And that was only one ship unwilling to pay for dockside garbage removal.

The tradewinds kicked into high gear and for several days we sat tucked behind a small island off the east end of Puerto Rico. But finally, we pulled the remaining thorns from our feet and sailed those last thirty miles to St. Thomas.

Ashore, a carnival was in progress. We'd like to think it was in honor of our arrival and chose to ignore the fact that it is a yearly event. Here, a quart of rum sold for 99 cents at the grocery store – party on!

"Up a river somewhere"
(with a paddle)

`The Big Turn West

" We do Rum. "

The Virgin Islands are anything but; deflowered years ago by the tourist trade. However, to this day the Virgins remain the Mecca for charter boats. Within the confines of the archipelago, the seas are flat even in the nastiest weather, eliminating, for the most part, mal-de-mer. Every bay has the requisite watering hole and eatery, from the casual thatched hut to four-star opulence. It is a great place to entertain company and that's what we did, on and off, for two months. No wonder the quest for the best Pina Colada in the Caribbean began here.

Our first visitors from New Mexico, Steve and Bonnie brought their windsurfing gear along and proceeded to zigzag their way through the U.S. and British Virgins alike. It was during their stay that we stumbled upon a cruiser's gold mine - especially cruisers on a budget. We were anchored in a quiet, palm-lined bay less than two miles from one of the major yacht charter companies. A birthday celebration rocked the cockpit of a chartered sailboat anchored nearby. When the birthday cake appeared, the four of us sang along with the six of them and were promptly invited over for a champagne toast. It was the last night out for these folks. They would fly back to the daily grind the next day and were poised close to the charter base for tomorrow's return. The party carried on for some hours and by then everyone knew of our world cruise agenda. When we made our departure move, they insisted on giving us all their leftover stores. When six people on holiday shop for ten days worth of groceries it is a substantial haul. And who, when there is a nice restaurant in every anchorage, is interested in galley duty? We couldn't believe our good fortune. This wasn't a few meager scraps; it was a month of food for Linda and me, from fresh fruit, cookies and gourmet sauces to canned chickens and hams. A place such as the Virgin Islands is definitely the mother-load, but the discovery paid great dividends in many places over the next ten years.

Linda's sister Nancy, and her cousin Nikki were the next to arrive. Our plan was to spend time in the Virgins then head for St. Martin – still a bit more easting. We left from the Bitter End Yacht Club on Virgin Gorda and set out across the Anegada Passage, a notorious forty miles of sloppy ocean. The wind had picked up and by 10 p.m. the sound of stomachs in distress competed with TR pounding eastward. Linda and I conferred and promptly turned to the southwest, laying a downwind course for St. Croix, the southernmost of the Virgin Islands.

Linda reveled in the company of her family. I hadn't seen her so happy in months. We got in some great diving on the reefs at Buck Island, one of the few aquatic parks in the Caribbean. One rainy day we toured the Cruzan Rum factory and wouldn't you know, it was Pina Colada day - good thing we'd taken a taxi.

Across the street form the rum factory, there was an immense organic chicken farm. We took the opportunity to stock up on ten dozen fresh unrefrigerated eggs. With a thin coat of Vaseline to seal the porous shell, fresh eggs will last up to six months. Refrigerated eggs last about half that time.

Nikki flew home and Nancy's boyfriend Gray flew in. He'd done some sailing before and was quite handy much to TR's delight – another slave to her vanity. We sailed back to the BVI to tackle the Anegada Passage again, stopping briefly to dive the wreck of the Rhone, an old mail ship lying in 80 feet of water. This time the passage was a pussycat, favoring us with a light north wind.

For two days, we feasted on seafood we'd caught on the reefs around Anguilla and then put in to Marigot Bay, the French side of St. Martin. While snorkeling in the outer anchorage, I found two abandoned anchors which were turned into cash and traded for a heavy duty 220 volt – 110 volt transformer which would enable me to use all my American power tools in the rest of the world.

Despite having her sister aboard, Linda felt compelled to fly home for what she deemed a much-needed break. This did not bode well for any long term sailing plans. But a 35-foot boat is a small place to live with discontent. I was sad to see her leave and could only hope she'd have an epiphany during her recess. I wouldn't see Linda again for four months.

Nancy, Gray and I island hopped over to St. Barts, getting clobbered by a tropical wave in the process. Forty knots of wind and torrential rain so intense that I had to wear my dive mask to see and breathe. Fortunately it only lasted an hour, but in those reef-strewn waters, an hour in zero visibility is a long time. St. Barts caters heavily to the jet set so the duty free wine and cheese shops had an impressive selection, all of which was surprisingly affordable.

While I grudgingly tolerated the actual sailing, Gray really loved it and was more of a purist than I ever would be. To this end, we rarely used the engine, opting instead to sail off the hook and anchor under sail. With a crew of three this was easily handled. TR wasn't exactly a dainty sailor; I likened her to the hippos dancing in Disney's Nutcracker Suite. She came alive in a stiff breeze and when her lightweight kin shortened sail, she demanded more. Fluky winds and crowded anchorages called for the engine. St. Barts was one such situation. We raised the main and motored up to the hook. As we started to weave our way through the crowd of yachts, TR's motor raced and quit. Out of fuel, we were on our own. Gray and Nancy had the staysail up in a flash but without a breeze the sails hung like so much wet laundry. To our good fortune, the tide was on the ebb and with a minimum of apologies and fending off, we were sucked unscathed out of the harbor. I'd failed to switch the fuel return valve to the proper tank. It took, and would always take, at least ten minutes to bleed the engine's fuel system of air before the beast would agree to start.

A pleasant downwind sail to Saba allowed us time to work on some of TR's cosmetics, scraping off old yellow paint and oiling the bare wood. Saba is a perfect cone jutting from the sea. Even close to, the anchorage was 60 feet deep. We set the fish trap and promptly caught a three-foot shark – what a fiasco. Ultimately I jerked the thing tail-first through the bait door. Waste Not – Want Not – we ate him. I hadn't yet learned about soaking the meat in vinegar to neutralize the ammonia smell. We didn't keep the leftovers.

Over 2000 stone steps challenged us to climb to Saba's summit, through two storybook Dutch villages, Top and Bottom respectively. Often clouded in, the summit treated us to a moment of clarity and six other islands came into view – spectacular! Our legs didn't think the hike was such a hot idea, treating us to sore quads for a week.

While spearfishing at the south end of St. Kitts, Gray and I came across a single coral head studded with over twenty lobster, nine of which we took back to the boat. I loved having a dive partner, especially when we foraged for food. If the water got a bit bloody, it was great to have someone looking out for sharks. Plus, a shared experience always seemed more fulfilling. I should mention that, other than the odd harmless nurse shark asleep on the bottom, I never saw a shark while diving in the Caribbean. The Pacific would be another story, but we hadn't gotten there yet.

After a brisk sail south to Montseratt, we fought our way through a barrage of downdrafts into an anchorage at the north end. Much to Gray's disappointment, we did this my way which was to drop all sails and motor in. Yes, I'm a bit lazy but those bullets of wind are hell on sails.

One look at a chart and you can see there would be little to no easting after reaching Antigua, our next stop. An all day sloppy beat put those last forty miles behind us and we crept into a quiet bay at dusk. Quiet that is until the disco on shore fired up at ten – a rude reminder that tourism is the major industry in the Caribbean.

To help celebrate this eastern landmark we'd caught and later grilled a ten-pound mackerel. Anytime TR was in deep water, the trolling line, aka meat hook, was in use. This is 100 yards of 1/8th inch nylon cord with ten 10 yards of 300lb. monofilament and 3 feet of heavy stainless steel leader attached to a large double hook. The bait was usually a colored plastic squid. The beauty of this rig is that the weakest point is the hook, which means if something like a freight train going the opposite direction hits the line, the hook straightens out and you haven't lost the rig – a big expense. Also, whatever it was that straightened the hook is not something you'd want aboard anyway.

Antigua is a huge yachting center with the infrastructure to support the international crowd. When Gray phoned home, there was a job prospect waiting that he couldn't pass up. I'd really enjoyed sailing with him and Nancy, but long-term sailing wasn't their dream. And Linda had no immediate plans to return. I was now confronted with the fact that it was only my dream. That meant single-handing, something I'd never quite envisioned myself doing. In my dream, I always had crew.

But a single-hander I was, and set about rigging TR for that purpose. Mostly this entailed re-routing sheet lines and halyards and fixing in place quite a number of tie-downs or as real sailors say, gaskets. What I soon realized was that single-handing was more a state of mind than anything else. It meant greater mental preparation and a different sequential approach to getting under way and anchoring. With crew, I'd merrily motor up to the anchor and once the crew had it secured, I would head into the wind while they hoisted sail. Now, however, I'd crank in half the chain, raise the mainsail and ready a foresail before bringing the anchor home, then move back to the helm and motor into unconfined space before raising the foresail. The snake in my guts made the first few forays out of the harbor a frantic undertaking, but after a few excursions I began to settle down and soon my actions took on a casual look – not that it ever really felt that way.

I spent a couple of weeks cruising the south coast of Antigua, using English Harbor as a base. Lord Nelson kept his fleet here in the early 1800s and now it's the home to a lot of fancy yachts. I pampered TR with new deck paint using ground walnut shells for a non-skid additive. The local chandlery had an extremely wide, albeit pricey, selection of equipment, mostly imported from England, and I was able to obtain some hard-to-find spares for TR's pumps, toilet and motor.

Then one day I got a little too cocky and almost lost the boat again. I was anchored in Falmouth Harbor, a large basin adjacent to English Harbor, when Sarah and Parker who I'd met in Haiti, invited me aboard for dinner. They were anchored in English Harbor, a ten-minute motor around the headland. I upped anchor, stowed it in the chocks, and cruised out of the harbor, not bothering to remove the mainsail cover. There wasn't much wind, but a heavy groundswell ran in from the east. TR had a pretty good roll to her as she pitched over the waves. I stood out a couple hundred yards and, even over the engine noise, heard the whump of those rollers when they broke against the rocky cliff. At the halfway point I detected a clatter within the diesel hum. Scanning the gauges, I was horrified to see no oil pressure. I madly unlatched the engine hatch and was immediately covered by a fine spray of black oil. The copper line to the oil pressure gauge had fractured just as it left the engine and most of TR's oil was now in the bilge. Under the circumstances I couldn't risk shutting down the engine, only lower the speed. The anchor was stowed on deck and the damn sail-cover was on – Murphy at his best. In a panic, I dove below and grabbed a pencil off the chart table and scrambled back into the cockpit. Reaching into the engine room, I jammed the pencil tip into the broken fitting hoping it would wedge itself in there and stop the leak. TR rolled sharply, I lunged for the wheel, brought her back on course, then tore into one of the cockpit lockers for the two quarts of oil I knew were there. Kneeling in the cockpit with one hand on the wheel and one pouring lifeblood into the engine I steered past the low reef at the entrance to English harbor and into calm water. It was clear I hadn't yet learned to think like a single-hander. I took that lesson to heart and since then have never left or entered harbor without sails up or an anchor poised to drop – crew or no crew.

The next two months I spent poking around the French Island of Guadeloupe, and the small islands just to the south, becoming a single-hander. TR and I holed up in a marina in Pointe a Pitre, the capital city, for the height of hurricane season where she got a complete makeover: a rich chocolate- brown topside paint, fresh varnish on her spars and a new bottom job.

It was here I was introduced to French wines and the four-hour lunch. I'd met a young French couple while sailing the west coast of Guadeloupe who told me to look them up if I made it to Pointe a Pitre. Fortunately they both spoke some English since my French was at this time nonexistent. When I called they invited me to Sunday lunch. Around noon I set aside the paintbrush thinking I'd be back around two and could finish varnishing the boom.

I cleaned up and had just stepped onto the jetty when a lovely brunette approached and asked me something in French, to which I answered with a blush, an apology and a shrug. She then held out a piece of paper and written on it was Fritz / Theodora R. "Whoa, that's me." Turned out Liz taught English at the local high school and my friends had sent her to fetch me, being to busy with food preparation. We stopped at a well-stocked wine shop where Liz instructed me in the basics of red table wine. I had to keep reminding myself that I was only a single-hander in the nautical sense. Life was getting complicated especially since Linda still hadn't set a return date. We didn't arrive at my friend's house until after one, where cocktails were just being served. The meal, four courses plus desert and different wine with each, followed by brandy and cigars carried on until six. An hour of loud rock music accompanied the cleanup. I hadn't had such a good time since Gray, Nancy and I had crashed a party aboard a windjammer cruise-ship. The varnish would have to wait.

I sailed south with a bilge stacked with wine and some new plastic shoes, a type I would wear for the next 8 years. I even had crew for the next leg, Tommy, a radical right-wing Texan who'd been taking care of the boat next to TR at the marina. We made a blustery overnight passage to Martinique, bypassing Dominica because of nasty winds and the open anchorage.

The one thing I missed on the French islands was English style rum. Tommy and I were complaining about it in a hotel bar that night, when the couple seated next to us leaned over and asked if we wanted some real rum. We followed them to their room where they opened a large suitcase packed with 24 bottles of Cockspurs Old Gold, the rum of choice for people from Barbados. These folks were on holiday for ten days, so when they said, "We do rum", I believed them. Drunk neat, it was indeed terrific rum. With our new rummy friends, we shared a car for an island tour. Martinique, like Guadeloupe, is a huge island and one day didn't really do the place justice, but we got a taste of its extreme terrain changes and wide spectrum of flora. Our Badjian friends then spent a couple days aboard TR working on their tan. That week is still a bit hazy, but I vaguely recall tottering around at great heights while varnishing the mast.

I sailed alone to St. Lucia and poked TR's bowsprit into all the different harbors, in advance of Linda's return and expected company. My mother Connie, her husband Jack and my brother

Chris, flew in for ten days. Their luggage contained a new outboard for the dinghy and a replacement engine for the generator – WOW early Xmas.

I picked them up at the south end of the island and we cruised north stopping to snorkel and fish. They stayed at a small inn in Marigot Bay, the ultimate hurricane hole with a lush tropical surround, and from there we explored the entire island and even slipped in an overnighter to Martinique for the French experience. I grew quite fond of Marigot Bay, and a few of the locals that worked or lived there. To this day, along with Clarencetown in the Bahamas, it is my favorite anchorage in the Caribbean

The day before the folks left, Linda arrived looking a bit white and pasty – nothing a few days in the sun wouldn't cure. It was great to have her back and she seemed pretty up about the voyage.

The next few weeks were totally hectic and I got a glimpse into the life of a charter captain. With three friends from New Mexico and two from Guadeloupe we sailed out of Martinique where we'd put in for supplies. Squally weather blew out the genoa again and forced us to hole up in a small cove at the south end of Martinique. With 7 people aboard, accommodation was tight, but we all survived. We dropped two of the crew at St. Lucia and cruised south toward St. Vincent and the Grenadines. At the Pitons, St. Lucia's answer to the Rio's Sugarloaf, fierce downdrafts required us to tie off to the palm trees ashore because we couldn't trust the anchors to hold in the steep shoreline.

St. Vincent turned out to be a fantastic provisioning spot, with a daily produce market that would challenge any artist's palette. It was a good thing we stocked up, the Grenadines had little to choose from and even that came from St. Vincent. That first day out, we spotted our first whale, a medium sized humpback, fifty feet from the boat. Two days later we were joined by a school of several hundred dolphin, who escorted TR for about a mile, entertaining us with wild aerial stunts and perfectly executed formation swimming. After a week of island hopping, the rest of the crew moved on to different agendas and Linda and I had TR to ourselves again.

The reprieve lasted one week, before my father Fred, and his buddy Bob, flew in from California for ten days. Linda slipped into another funk, trying to come to terms with the extended voyage and how it would ultimately affect her own desires and career plans. Fortunately, neither of us had been keen on having children and I had gone as far as having a vasectomy soon after we'd married. The more I traveled, the more I liked it so with her blessings we deferred a final decision until reaching Panama. That was only a few months away and Linda felt she could easily handle that. Her spirits rose and never flagged again.

We ducked back into St. Vincent, picked up Fred and Bob, another load of fresh produce and shot back to Bequia, the northernmost of the Grenadines. At the time, Bequia residents still harpooned whales from sailing skiffs, although they'd only taken two whales in as many years. Bequia is also a center for cruising boats with its accommodating bay and merchants centrally located in the Windward Islands. All around the world I was to hear the departing phrase, "See you in Bequia for Christmas."

Within days, Fred and Bob were suitably grizzled and had taken to the cruising life, especially the torn shorts and T-shirt part. Getting in and out of the dinghy, however, did present a minor challenge, but after they'd sunk it a couple times, the chore of bailing it out encouraged them to use caution.

On a back street in Cariacou, Fred and I heard an odd tinking sound coming from behind a dense hedge. On investigation, we found a man tuning a newly fabricated steel drum. It was fascinating to watch him shape the squares to the proper pitch all of which he did by instinct and ear using a small hammer. He'd been making steel drums all his life and was quite the master.

With guests aboard, galley duty was on rotation. When it was Fred or Bob's turn, it meant the nearest restaurant. In this way we sampled a wide variety if native foods and tested more Pina Coladas. We even found a rum-shack on Mayreau, a quaint island still operating in the 19th century that served grilled fish filets. Where the wood came from for the fire is a mystery.

The Grenadines are similar to the Bahamas in that they are predominantly low-lying and surrounded by turquoise water and numerous reefs. I dove with some locals on Thanksgiving Day and brought back a large triggerfish and some lobster for the feast. Nobody missed the turkey.

In a classic Windward Island reach, we sailed the length of Granada and put in at St. George, the quintessential Caribbean harbor town with rows of gingerbread colonial buildings in rainbow colors climbing the tropic hillside. Politically Granada was still under Cuban / Russian control. It was the first place we were confronted with armed soldiers on the street and around the civil buildings. A serious jetport was under construction southwest of town and when Russian ships came in with supplies, the whole island was under strict curfew until the ships left port. Fred and Bob, both of the cold war generation, were understandably skeptical about the situation. But the only thing they really had to worry about was the cab ride to the airport for their flight home. A toothless prune of a man in a rusted out Fiat with brakes that required constant pumping gave us a white-knuckle ride up steep snaking canyons to the mountain valley that held the airstrip. We all sighed with relief at our safe arrival. The pisser was, I had to ride back down.

It was the only trip my father made on TR, but the Grenadines was his only dream and I was glad that I could help make it a reality. We would miss him.

We celebrated Christmas and New Years among other yachties, feasting aboard a German yacht Christmas Day and providing guitar accompaniment for a beach party sing-along on the 31st. The tropical Christmas was a first for Linda and me, but the absence of snow and frosty breath were no match for the hard-drivin' holiday spirit blasting from boom-boxes everywhere. Rasta Claus is a sure cure for the Christmas blues.

Early in the morning of 1983 we made the big turn west and sailed, for the first time in ten months, into the sunset. The islands off the coast of Venezuela were our first objective for two reasons, cheap fuel and lobster. At 30 cents a gallon, we could top up TR for 15 dollars. She held 30 gallons in tanks and 20 in jugs at the stern. Her 35-hp BMC diesel burned about ¾ of a gallon an hour, which gave us a 300-mile range at 5 knots. This proved to be adequate for all but the vast distances in the Pacific, Indian and Atlantic oceans.

As for the lobster, well, that's kind of embarrassing. I'd plotted a course to Los Roques from the west end of Isla Margarita, but must have overcompensated for the current, because by late afternoon when that cluster of islands should have appeared over the bow, there was nothing but open water. The wind had risen to a solid 20 knots, so we eased the sheets and ran due west hoping to come down on our target. An hour before sunset, TR rose high on a swell and I caught a glimpse of Los Roques, about ten miles off and well astern. In those seas there was no going back. We blew it off and hoped for better luck with Las Aves.

With a fairly accurate fix off Los Roques, we expected to raise the light on Las Aves around midnight. Las Aves is mostly low-lying coral reefs, so if the light didn't appear as planned, we would alter course to give it a wide berth. But the light did appear and we skirted the south end and sailed into the lee. I had expected flatter seas than we encountered in the lee, making the easterly approach a bit chaotic. When the depth sounder read 30-feet, I let go the anchor. I waited for the chain to slow its passage once the anchor hit bottom, but it kept up a mad pace right to the bitter end. Puzzled I checked the depth sounder again. It still read 30-feet, but the 150-feet of chain with a 65 pound plow anchor attached hung vertical. That was a lot of weight to crank up on TR's windlass. By the time I'd retrieved the ground tackle, I was exhausted and in no mood to keep messing around in potentially dangerous waters at night. We saluted the lobster, hoisted sail and flew off downwind.

Bonaire provided the first quiet anchorage since Granada, and gave us a chance to rehab a variety of gear that had taken a beating during our first downwind jaunt. We'd chaffed through two sets of sheet lines and one halyard. On further inspection, I found the masthead fitting and a shackle bent severely out of shape. I definitely had to figure out a better way to rig TR's headsails.

The coral walls around Bonaire made it a world class dive destination, and the nature preserve held a tremendous flock of pink flamingos. These we saw to some extent but what sticks in my mind is my first encounter with the yacht Cambria, a 120-foot ex J-boat that had been entirely refurbished at a shipyard in the Canary Islands five years earlier. Now, instead of a single 140-foot mast, she sported a ketch rig with a 100-foot main and slightly smaller mizzen all in highly varnished spruce. As a guitar maker, I was especially interested in the spruce, because five years earlier

I'd made a special trip to a lumberyard in California specifically to buy spruce and cedar for soundboards. A week before my visit, the yard had shipped almost all its high quality spruce to the Canary Islands to be used for Cambria's new spars. When I met the owner, Mike Sears, I told him the story. He laughed and almost went as far as extending me an apology, but I assured him he'd made excellent use of the wood.

The only attraction in Aruba was gambling, and that was brief. After I'd sold my guitar business I had taught myself how to count cards and spent long weekends in Las Vegas at the blackjack tables to pass the time. I actually made several hundred dollars on each outing but it was a lot of work. This was before there were non-smoking tables. So in Aruba, on a whim, I took twenty dollars to the casino, returning in less than an hour flat broke.

In Curacao I was, with some tricky halyard work, able to remove the masthead fitting. I took this into the industrial part of town and found a machine shop equipped to handle the repair. I also discovered, since leaving Bonaire, that polished bronze does not chafe the running gear, giving new life to all TR's lines.

Curacao is also a major fueling station for cruise ships and freighters. At one point we found ourselves in the commercial harbor where a cruise liner was taking on fuel. There were five pumping stations, each with four large hoses, like tentacles, attached to the ship. I approached one of the stations and heard a steady click, click, click, about one per second, coming from the pump. I asked the attendant what the clicks were. He said each click represented one cubic meter of fuel. The ship was attached to the pumps for hours.

Our next passage, three days, to the San Blas Islands, was the longest to date. The second day out we encountered monster swells where the Atlantic rollers felt the north shelf of Columbia. TR would rise at the stern until, with the decks tilted to forty degrees, we sighted down the face of the wave four full boat lengths to the trough, some 150-feet. Luckily they weren't steep enough to break, although the frothy tops would occasionally tumble and drench whomever was at the helm – what a sleigh ride.

On our second night, not far from the Colombian coast, we noticed the lights of a fishing trawler a couple of hundred yards to starboard. At first we paid it no mind, but after several hours passed and it was still in the same place, it began to wear on our nerves. Thoughts of drug runners and pirates made sleep impossible. But sometime near daybreak the boat drifted off.

The San Blas are ringed by a barrier reef making a daylight approach a must. At midnight of the third day, 20 miles out, we hove to by backing the foresail, sheeting the main in tight and lashing the helm hard to port. We rocked comfortably on the sea with a one-knot drift to the west. Bright moonlight gave us a clear horizon so I was able to use the sextant to shoot Saturn, the moon and two stars for a reliable position fix. At dawn we sailed southwest for three hours, cleared the reef and anchored behind a small island in ten feet of clear water over bright white sand.

The Cuna Indians exist in a matriarchal society and after one trip ashore it was clear that the women ran the show, delegating domestic chores to the men. In all business matters, we dealt with Mom. These no-nonsense ladies are probably best known for making molas, a colorful reverse applique textile used to decorate their blouses. Designs for the molas were no longer limited to Mayan motifs. Harley Davidson, and Santa Claus now claimed their market share. When I passed through in 1974, a used mola went for fifty cents. I now gladly paid thirty-five dollars for the same.

My sister Carla flew in for a couple weeks of R and R. Seafood on the reef was plentiful and lots of creative dishes came from the galley, lobster crepes being an all time favorite. Of the 400 islands comprising the San Blas, we limited our cruising to a dozen then headed for the canal. We spent one night in Puerto Bello where a local restaurant served us the special of the day, iguana − tastes like rattlesnake.

The port of Colon on the Atlantic side of Panama had cleaned up the oil slicks in the harbor since my last visit, but the crime rate had skyrocketed. We tied stern-to at the yacht club, protected by a high chain-link fence. Muggings in town were almost a daily occurrence and we never ventured out alone. I always carried a three-cell Maglite strapped to my wrist to discourage possible attacks.

Carla couldn't stay for the canal transit and bid her farewell after a wild night in town where highly costumed locals celebrated the Day of the Dead. The three of us faced off a number of goulish confrontations, but in the end it was all in fun.

Linda and I now had to confront our own issues. Linda had had enough of the sailing life, and the Pacific and its long passages was no place for a negative attitude, especially on a small boat. I, on the other hand, had already made the mental leap into new waters.

The Caribbean was meant as a shakedown cruise and TR had proven herself capable, but not so Linda and me. We discussed the possibility of a fly-in fly-out relationship, but agreed that considering the distances and cost it was impractical. For the first time we spoke of divorce. We couldn't help but think of it as admitting failure but as Linda pointed out, our wedding vows were about encouraging growth in each other. Our voyages, sad as it seemed, would take different paths. Linda would stay for the canal transit then travel north through Central America with a new lady friend. These days when speaking with others about my voyage I am frequently asked what I considered to be my worst experience. It was unquestionably the breakup of our marriage.

I posted "crew wanted" signs in the yacht club and took on a project building a master suite in the hold of an old wood fishing trawler. The owner, an old German ship captain said he wanted to smuggle women in from Columbia. I hope he was kidding. I figured it would take a couple of weeks and give me plenty of time to find crew. Plus, we could use the extra cash.

Crew showed up a week later in the form of a young French couple, Olivier and Isabel, who had just arrived from Columbia (their first stop on a world tour) where they'd been forced at gunpoint to strip naked in an alley and had all their worldly possessions stolen. As you can imagine it had been a thoroughly humiliating and frightening experience but they maintained an amazingly buoyant attitude. Luckily they'd been able to get more travel money wired from home. Olivier stood over six feet and much to my delight, was a chef. Isabel was petite and spoke excellent English which more than made up for Olivier's lack of the language. She would prove to have an uncanny touch at the helm. I left most of the provisioning to Olivier since he had happily agreed to cook. How we found room for all the Cote du

Rhone I'll never know.

I finished the work on the trawler in record time and was immediately besieged with requests for all sorts of building projects from house additions to new yacht construction. If I hadn't been set on a world cruise, I'd still be in Panama.

March 18th, transit day, arrived. We took on our pilot and joined a French ketch that would share center chamber with TR behind a 300-foot freighter. The ketch had lines to their side of the lock and TR had lines to her side of the lock then we were attached by two 25-foot lines. As the lock filled or emptied we adjusted the tension on our respective lock lines to keep us in the center of the chamber.

At the first lock, all went well until the freighter ahead of us powered up to move forward. The prop-wash spun our two vessels like so much flotsam. The ¾" nylon lines stretched to half inch and water poured from the stressed braid. An oak samsonpost (a short post for tying off lines) in TR's cockpit couldn't handle the strain. With a loud crack it snapped off and shot across the lock. Luckily nobody was in its way. The pilot yelled something into his radio and the freighter backed off the power. A quick move by Olivier got the stray line around a winch and we managed to keep TR from smashing into the ketch. After that first lock, we went in front of the freighter.

The first time I'd transited the canal in 1974, I knew nothing of its creation and realized I'd missed out on a good part of the adventure. But this time I came educated and could marvel at the Culebra Cut where American ingenuity had sliced through the backbone of the Cordieras, Panama's central mountain range. I watched in awe as the massive, French engineered lock doors opened and closed with clock-like precision after 75-years of continuous use.

After the first three locks raised us over a hundred feet, we motored across Gatun Lake, the central portion of the canal and the source of water used to recharge the locks. I could only hope the Panamanian Government realized the surrounding rain forest was the ultimate source of water for the canal. We met severe turbulence again when the final doors swung wide at 3 p.m. and history was made as TR, for the first time in her 47 years, entered the Pacific Ocean. I considered the $75 transit fee a real bargain. To fully appreciate the miracle of the Canal, I encourage anyone to read the book, Path Between the Seas.

We dropped our pilot at the Balboa Yacht Club, a dicey maneuver due to four-foot swells rolling into the mooring area, and sailed to an anchorage at a nearby island. From here I escorted Linda back, via ferry and railway, to Colon where in heartfelt celebration we spent our final night together. I'll spare you the teary goodbye of the following day. Suffice to say it was a long lonely ride back to the boat. There was a certain amount of relief mixed with the sadness and regret. I'd been carrying around a lot of tension in anticipation of Linda's decision. That was a hard knot I was glad to untie.

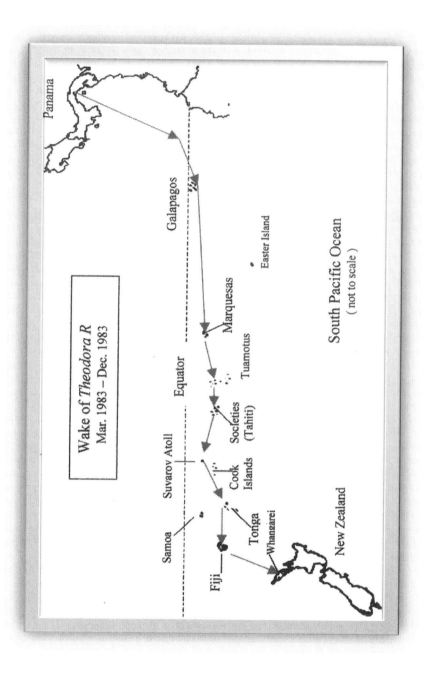

Into the Big Blue

"Don't listen to them, they're all in my hospital."

Moments after my return to the boat, a wind shift forced us out of the anchorage, a welcome distraction to my emotional turmoil. In a rare show of sympathy from Mother Nature, it was a favorable breeze for the short passage to the Las Perlas Islands, sixty miles south. I wanted to cruise this area for a week or so to familiarize the new crew with TR and her captain. I also wanted to make sure neither of them suffered from seasickness or had some hidden personality quirk that would make life aboard impossible. I was still close enough to the mainland to take them back without problem. When Olivier and I first met, he was smoking a cigarette. I'd asked him how important that was to him, because there was no way I'd take on crew who smoked. He'd assured me it would be no problem.

Fourteen-foot tides in the area allowed us to use TR's beaching legs, adjustable iron pipes that bolted to her sides at midship, keeping her upright as she rested on her keel. We eased, bow first, onto the sloping sand just past high tide so we'd be sure to float off on the next tide. It wouldn't do to get caught high and dry until the next full moon. As the water receded we scrubbed the hull then applied two coats of antifouling paint to protect TR's wood planking from marine borers which were a serious threat in the warm waters of the Pacific. Twelve hours later we were afloat. That night a freak thunderstorm clocked the wind and almost drove TR ashore before we fled and found a safe anchorage. The midnight anchor drill gave the crew a wicked little taste of what to expect form the elements – surprises.

I dove on a reef of submerged rock the next day. After the crystal waters of the Caribbean, these murky conditions gave me the willies. Moments after I jumped in, large shadows closed in from several directions. The shadows became sharks and my heart all but stopped. I didn't have the experience yet to coexist with these guys – I bolted. Besides, there was some brass on board that required polishing.

That afternoon, a fisherman came by in a small skiff and asked if we wanted to see his village. I couldn't leave the boat in such an exposed anchorage, Isabel didn't trust the guy's boat, but Olivier opted to go. I told Olivier to take some money in case there were some fresh vegetables to be had. We watched them putt over the horizon, which is about 3 miles from TR's deck. I had no idea where he'd gone, but there were only a couple islands out there. At dark we started to worry. I kept the masthead light on and crossed my fingers. An hour later we heard the sound of a small outboard approaching. It was the fisherman with a highly intoxicated Olivier. My crew scrambled aboard and the fisherman tossed up a large plastic sack, waved then disappeared in the dark. Curious, I opened the sack thinking cabbage or lettuce. It was greens all right, the heavy scent of marijuana wafted out and my entire college career flashed before me. Between bouts of laughter Olivier told about his adventure, culminating with the purchase of a whole kilo of Panama Red for five dollars. I had mixed feelings about having pot on board, but at five bucks a kilo I could see the temptation. Since we were leaving for the Galapagos in the morning, I asked him to lock it up with his cigarettes and that we'd probably have to dump it overboard. I never dreamed the dope would actually do some good. After all, the only thing bad about pot is that it's illegal in most places, so as the captain, I risked getting busted and possible jail time and/or losing the boat.

The snake returned with a vengeance as we prepared to make sail for the Galapagos. This would be my first true open-water passage and a real test of my navigational skills. The days of inexpensive, push-button GPS navigation equipment was 20 years in the future. I'd taught myself the basics of celestial navigation from a small booklet written by a man named Kitteridge, a straightforward cookbook approach that provided the essentials. I looked forward to the challenge and would refine my technique as the years passed. Sat Navs had just come on the market, the electronics proving to be somewhat unreliable. Picking up their signals from orbiting satellites, hours would pass between fixes. The three to five thousand-dollar price tag also convinced me to go with a sextant and HO249 sight reduction tables used by early airplane navigators. I also used a portable AM radio as a radio direction finder by tuning in a local station and pointing the end of the ferrite rod in its handle toward the signal. When the signal faded out, I would check the direction against a compass and that was the line of position. I'd met an old Swede in Panama single-handing around the world. His boat was an old 32-foot sloop whose wooden mast had been broken and repaired countless times and looked like a mosaic. He now sailed everywhere with only a reefed main and small jib. He carried two transistor radios, one cheap and one expensive. On a long passage he would sail in the general direction of his destination unit he thought he was within 300 miles of landfall, then turn on the expensive radio until he picked up a commercial station. That's when he knew he had to watch for shipping in the area. In a couple of days he would turn on the cheap radio. When that one picked up the signal he knew he was very close and must stay awake. He'd been at it for over ten years.

The other issue was water. TR carried 70 gallons in two bronze tanks and ten gallons in jugs on deck. Back in Colon, in a moment of doubt, I had loaded twenty gallon jugs of drinking water that were being thrown out by the guy whose boat I'd worked on. These were stuffed in every nook and cranny. Crossing the ocean was not much different than crossing a desert, just a bit cooler. Our fresh water combined with canned or bottled beverages seemed like plenty, but how was I to know? All my experience to date were short trips, confident there would be a hose on the dock when I got there. Being overcautious I tried to impress on the crew the value of our fresh water supply and even told them to use seawater to brush their teeth. I recall Olivier's give-me-a-break look and saying, "But Fritz it is so little." Little or not, I would be overly strict until I could judge water needs on a passage.

TR had both fresh water and salt-water foot pumps servicing the galley sink. We used the salt water for everything except drinking and some cooking. Steaming instead of boiling rice and vegetables kept fresh water use to a minimum for cooking.

The sailing directions for tall ships leaving Panama for the Galapagos advised dropping south to just north of the equator for a westerly approach. This was, of course, assuming normal tradewind conditions. But this was an El Nino year and the warm water of this reverse current running across the Pacific had the weather patterns in total confusion. Unfortunately I hadn't given the ramifications of this condition enough thought and followed the printed advice. Luckily, my tendency to lay a direct course whenever possible put us several hundred miles further west when we ran out of wind. The run down had been a comfortable reach and Bill had steered most of the way. After one full day of complete lull, the sails hanging like wet laundry, a light breeze filled from, yes, the west. We started our upwind climb, tacking at every 4-hour watch change. I shot a round of stars the first evening and plotted our position. If I were to believe my navigation, we had drifted backwards ten miles - the snake in my guts snickered. I reworked the sights over and over and at midnight finally got it that the El Nino was working against us. Four days of sailing later we had held our loss to fifty miles. A brisk wind from the north finally gave us a break and in three days we were only 50 miles out. The wind increased to gale force and we closed the gap to 25 miles before conditions worsened forcing us to heave-to. TR rode the rising swells like a fat lady in a Jacuzzi. Now and then a wave would break over her bow and green water poured from her decks.

In dead calm at daybreak we began motoring toward Isla Santa Cruz, a huge island thousands of feet in elevation. At noon, the moon was still out so I was able to get a reliable fix that put us 20 miles out. Once again I began to doubt my navigation - the snake chuckled. Surely we should be able to see such a big land mass at twenty miles on a clear day. I reworked the numbers several times with no change. My crew started giving me odd looks – not good. At five miles out I stood on TR's bowsprit and stared forward with such intensity that out of the mist a shoreline appeared, then houses, then boats at anchor and great relief. (Did I mention that I'm real big on visualization techniques?). We'd been sailing for days enshrouded by thick misty conditions and never realized our visibility didn't extend beyond the 3-mile horizon.

All the pictures I'd seen of the Galapagos had been barren moonscapes on a parched land, so when the lush green jungle of Isla Santa Cruz appeared, the dramatic affects of El Nino started to sink in. Unprecedented rainfall had reformed the islands, driving off or killing much of the natural fauna and sea life. The cold water of the Humbolt current that generally flowed here was hundreds of feet below, smothered by the warm water of El Nino. Without a special cruising visa that I'd tried unsuccessfully to obtain, we were only allowed to stay 5 days. Despite incessant rain, we crammed a lot into that five days, touring the Darwin Institute, probing the overgrown roadways inland to see the giant tortoises and iguanas. Off-road hiking was impossible, even with a machete. I met a fellow guitar player, Ade Matson, who was there on a grant to study El Nino. Besides playing lots of music together, I went out in his skiff to help set special submerged equipment for measuring the speed and temperature of the current. In places the current ran up to 8 knots with water temperatures in the high 80s.

A daily flight from Ecuador, brought in plenty of fresh produce and meats. One night Olivier produced an amazing feast for all the folks at the Darwin Institute, taking over their kitchen for an entire day. They were sorry to see us leave.

I managed to top up our diesel tanks and one of the propane tanks mounted on the stern. Olivier used the oven (a real gas hog) more than Linda and I ever did, so we burned propane much faster than before. We used to get about 3 months out of one tank and now it was half that. But I never regretted the casseroles and breads coming from the galley. I did introduce Olivier to the pressure cooker, which reduced gas use by speeding up cooking time for many dishes.

We sailed for the Marquesas, 3000 miles away, in a blustery rainsquall, the loamy scent of land escorting us all the way to the equator. The equatorial crossing was another first for all of us including TR. Bill had the helm and the wind blew softly from the east. Olivier outdid himself in the galley, serving braised beef medallions under a white wine sauce, steamed mixed vegetables smothered in spiced cheese, baked potatoes and creme brulee for desert. From the cockpit we toasted Poseidon with red wine as the sun melted into blushing cloud-cover.

Dreams of consistent tradewinds driving us merrily across the waves were soon dashed as El Nino conjured up flukey winds from around the compass. Sail changes were sometimes an hourly task. Twice during the 28-day passage huge glassy swells rolled in from the northeast, evidence of storm conditions somewhere in the far distance. We could only hope that whatever it was, wasn't coming our way. The conditions were especially hard on the sails and the sewing machine became a permanent fixture on the dining table. Eventually, as we dropped south, the trades made themselves felt and the days rolled into a pleasing routine. I put aside a novel I was reading to write the following song that basically summed up our days. I don't recall the melody now but it works as a poem.

Long Passage Routine

It's an hour before sunrise and the sky's turnin' gray
The waves show their faces as they look for the day
Distant clouds take on shapes as the stars fade away
And the boat surges on in the foam and salt spray

Hot coffee from the galley takes the chill off the dawn
The helm changes hands when the night has withdrawn
Clothes are all shed as the sun shows its brawn.
And the sails are changed if the wind's comin' on

The sun is our guide as it passes high noon
Anxious for landfall we speculate how soon
Hot bread from the oven on which goodies are strewn
A new face at the wheel whistles a tune

A bit of painting and some sail repair
The chef begins thinking of a sauce for tonight's fare
A rum punch at 5 mixed with great care
Helps smooth ruffled feathers but these are quite rare

In awe of the sunset we eat the cook's pride
Sometimes interrupted by a squall's wild ride
A change of watch and we linger outside
Then a last daylight check to be sure lines are tied

Venus emerges as darkness arrives
Constellations form from the stars they comprise
With tools of the trade and the stars blinkin' eyes
We find our position so land is no surprise

The wee hours are here and the watch is renewed
No ships have been sighted and the course is reviewed
Sometimes it's rainin' but this won't spoil our mood
And a new day begins as the coffee is brewed.

At the point of no return, 1500 miles from any land and the water 4 miles deep, we went for a swim. Afloat on the surface, the sunrays seemed to shine down into infinity. I found it very difficult if not downright impossible not to imagine a huge set of jaws rising out of the deep. We were probably the smallest morsels out there for most of the fish cruising by. Isabel lasted about ten seconds but Olivier and I toughed it out long enough to knock the gooseneck barnacles off the hull. I'd been surprised to find quite a number up to two inches long clustered just below the waterline.

Olivier had accepted no refrigeration without comment and I had weaned myself off cold beer long ago. Fresh produce lasted weeks; cabbage going for up to 3 months provided the stuff hadn't been refrigerated which is the case around most of the world. Vacuum packed cheese suffered a bit of oil separation but was otherwise fine. All condiments lasted indefinitely, including mayonnaise, as long it wasn't contaminated with canned tuna or the like. Beans, rice, pasta, flour, onions and potatoes were our major staples, plus Olivier was the master of sauces.

Three weeks into the passage, we ran out of butter – a serious predicament for our French chef. It was a good thing we had plenty of red wine to flush out the cholesterol. Necessity being the mother of invention, I dabbled with existing ingredients until we had a reasonable facsimile – one cup of Crisco, ¼ cup honey and a teaspoon of salt. When whipped together it excelled in baked goods. On toast, well.... All that really mattered was Olivier's contentment. He'd kept his word about the cigarettes so I felt obliged to reduce his anxieties.

I'd read stories about long passages where once the sails had been set up, weeks would go by without touching a line and books could be read by the armful. But now I'm skeptical. I think those tales are right up there with sailing off into the sunset drinking mint juleps in the cockpit. The sailing part was proving to be a hell of a lot of work and I'd not even made it through one book. Mind you, this isn't a complaint, just an observation.

Our electric power needs were minimal, the odd light and stereo. Later I would build a wind generator. Although efficient, it would prove to be too cumbersome for comfort with its 4 ft. prop whirring at deadly speed over the foredeck. Ultimately, I would settle on a single 45-watt solar panel, totally silent and no moving parts.

I felt the presence of land long before it appeared. The sea took on a different character, sort of a mild confusion rippling through the long Pacific swells. Seabirds swooped over the waves, we had a fish on the line, our first since leaving the Galapagos.

Then, on May 9th, the green volcanic spires of Nuku Hiva rose from the South Pacific right where I expected to see them.

After a month of solitude the twenty yachts at anchor seemed like quite a crowd, but the wide bay had plenty of swing room. Our nearest neighbors, Carl and Judy from Florida, rowed over and welcomed us with two gorgeous grapefruit. We would soon learn what an extravagant gift this was. They warned us of the no-nos ashore − noseeums with a nasty bite − and suggested long pants and shirts. Isabel would have none of it and dressed in short-shorts and tank-top. Later, we would count over 500 bites on her exposed flesh. She was bedridden and miserable for a week.

Fresh fruit and vegetables are usually a priority after a month at sea and after a cursory clearing in, we hit the shops only to find El Nino had been there before us. Two out-of-season hurricanes had kept the supply boats from leaving Papeete and torrential rains had washed out most of the native gardens. The locals carefully hoarded what fresh food there was, and the twenty yachts had scooped up what might have been for sale. The local bakery had the only flour and rightly so. At least we were able to get fresh baguettes. I was intrigued when Olivier bought a large chocolate bar and stuffed it into a hunk of bread. I followed his lead and with chocolate sandwiches in hand we set out to discover the extent of our deprivation. The only thing we found that might be considered a deterrent to scurvy was a single can of sliced peaches. Was it my imagination or were my teeth feeling loose?

The effects of Isabel's no-no bites didn't show up until that night. Welts popped up all over her body, the itching extreme. Rum and Benadryl bought her fitful sleep for the next week.

Fully clothed, Olivier and I hiked inland the next day. What passed for roads were so washed out and overgrown it was difficult to even walk. The dense odor of rotting vegetation permeated the air. At the end of one such track we came to a whitewashed frame house on short stilts with a tin roof set in a large clearing. On the front steps were several woodcarvings with a Polynesian Tiki theme. A young girl in a flowered sarong came outside at our approach. She pointed to the carvings and spoke to us in rapid French. At first it was obvious she was trying to sell the carvings, but then the conversation drifted in a new direction and I heard the word leprosy. I wanted to interrupt for a translation but forced myself to wait it out. That's when I heard a scuffling sound come from under the house. I watched, fascinated, as a bandaged hand gripped the weathered rail and an old man in tattered clothes crawled from under the steps. He stood next to the girl, stroked her head and smiled. Then I noticed the bandages were actually rags that poorly covered missing digits. An ear and part of his nose looked as though they had been chewed off. The leper didn't speak French so the girl translated for him and Olivier kept asking questions. Why couldn't I have taken French instead of Spanish in high school?

Eventually, Oliver said something about returning, grabbed my arm and we walked off. Turns out the old man was the girl's grandfather. He was also the woodcarver and owner of the house. But because of the leprosy, his family made him live under the house. The Tikis were ten dollars each but the old man had asked if we had any marijuana to trade because it is the only thing that stops his pain. Well... We were back at the house in two hours with a one pound sack of dope. I think the old man had expected a joint or two because for a minute there, considering his condition, I thought his eyes would literally pop out of his head. Olivier and I each chose a Tiki but granddad wouldn't hear of it. He ushered us to what I thought was just a cleared area behind the house but was actually an incredible garden that he and his granddaughter tended and somehow managed to save from the heavy rains. He handed us a plastic gunnysack then shuffled down the rows picking tomatoes, green peppers, eggplant and lettuce, onions and whatever else was ready to harvest. When the load became unmanageable he sent us on our way saying we were welcome to more anytime. No scurvy for us.

Two days later the first of the Chinese trading ships came in from Papeete. Sacks of flour, canned butter, eggs, corned beef, cabbage heads and potatoes were stacked high on the jetty, then, like a magic act, vanished into town.

During our stay, a French yacht came in from Panama with a young couple and a cat on board. They were both near death from starvation/scurvy and only survived by eking out the cat's food – lucky cat. On a previous trip from Panama, they had had strong tradewinds and made the trip in less than twenty days. This time, with thirty days food, they dropped to the equator for the run west and found no wind and El Nino. The passage took 123 days. After hearing their story, I never worried about an overstocked pantry.

We cruised to a spectacular bay on the west end of Nuku Hiva, complete with the classic waterfall into the lagoon, but the no-nos were so bad we couldn't get off the boat and Olivier would row around in the dinghy to smoke his cigarettes. On the north shore, we found an anchorage with very clear water and the diving excellent. Most other places had a stream or river mucking up the water inshore. Sharks were constant companions and I was never far from the dinghy, but after a while I could sense from their behavior if I was wearing out my welcome.

Moving south, we put in at Ua Pou long enough to catch the Friday night disco. Isabel, fully recovered and dressed like a mid-eastern peasant, made up for lost time and danced the night away. Olivier and I cashed it in at midnight.

We met a French doctor at the local clinic and quizzed him about ciguatera fish poisoning, a vile toxin that attacks the nervous system. It was prevalent in the area and we'd understood that the locals could tell us which fish were safe to eat. The doc laughed at that and said his hospital was full of those people. His advice was to always test the liver from the fish. If the liver sank in salt water then it was okay, if it floated it was infected. The liver should also look and feel like healthy liver tissue and taste sweet (if you're game enough to take a nibble). I've used his advice to this day and have never contracted ciguatera, but then I've never come across a floating liver.

A fierce thunderstorm forced us to abandon our anchorage at Ua Pou. We sailed for the Tuomotus aka the Dangerous Archipelago, so called because this extensive chain is comprised of low coral atolls beset by powerful tidal currents. Precise navigation was a must and I felt up to the challenge.

During this 4-day passage an incident occurred that would terminally alter my relationship with the crew. Early on I had instructed them both on the proper method for bucketing water from a moving vessel, emphasizing not to wrap the line around their hand. Isabel forgot this and was almost yanked overboard, abrading her hand and wrenching her shoulder. The bucket was history. Being somewhat attached to that bucket (as one gets on boats) I got angry about the lost bucket instead of showing concern for Isabel's physical condition, which in retrospect of course I should have done. Angry words were exchanged but we didn't harp on it and I thought it would blow over.

Takaroa didn't appear as expected. Again I found myself standing on TR's spreaders willing land to appear, which it eventually did and just where it was supposed to. El Nino spawned hurricanes had stripped the tall palm trees of all their fronds reducing the atolls visibility to 5 miles. These atolls usually have a narrow entrance on the leeward side, passable only at slack tide. The tide was in full ebb, so we tied to a battered copra jetty just outside the pass to wait.

The chief, his wife and two young daughters came aboard to welcome us and I soon found myself strumming the guitar to Home on the Range and a few gospel tunes. Homespun entertainment was losing ground to pool halls and videos on these outer atolls but families still seemed tight knit groups. The two daughters took Isabel aside and taught her the basic techniques for Polynesian tamare dancing where the hips move like they are attached to a vibrator.

I noticed a pack of around 15 dogs ranging across the reefs as the tide dropped. The chief explained that the dogs fed themselves from the reef and the villagers ate the dogs. Even pigs were hard to feed on some of the atolls where all that grew were coconut palms for the copra meat and a few root crops like tarot and manioc.

We entered the lagoon, another first, at slack tide, but the dogleg at the end created a whirlpool that swung TR close to a coral shelf. Inside was flat calm but fairly deep. We anchored in 60 feet of water close to some lone coral heads that promised good diving. We dined on fresh grouper that night. We were the only yacht there and that was the case 3 days later when we left. Remember that whirlpool in the dogleg in the pass? This time it grabbed TR and set her to spin as we drifted out the pass. I'd been told by a yachtie in Panama not to use engine power to control the spin, as this would make you slam into the coral walls of the pass. It took all my willpower to keep my hands off the controls, but we twirled out the pass unscathed.

Apataki is one of the larger atolls, some 20 miles across, but the main village offered a well-protected anchorage. Hurricanes had knocked out the icehouse depriving us of cold beer and the village of anything that required refrigeration. Olivier met up with a local fisherman his age and we invited him to cruise the atoll with us. For a week Marc guided us through the outer motus (small islands within the atoll) and showed us how to spot octopus and lobster. He was also adept at living in the bush, using local plants as utensils. He taught me how to climb coconut trees using only hands and feet, but when I reached the top of an eighty-footer I froze and had to shinny down, scraping the skin from my inner arms and thighs, the Polynesian equivalent of road-rash. I sported those scabs for a month.

Marc's spear gun was fashioned from a 6 foot shaft of mahogany and used a single long rubber band to launch the 7 foot spear. He would dive to the sandy bottom and lay still about 15 feet from a promising coral head. After 30 seconds had passed, the fish would come out from hiding and as soon as one swam in front of Marc's spear –TWANG – dinner. I found that successful spearfishing was totally a mind control exercise similar to meeting women in bars. If you were in the water intent on killing something, the fish were nowhere to be found.

We bid Marc farewell and set sail for Tahiti, the heart of Polynesia. The 3-day sail went without a hitch until dawn of the third day. We were ten miles out, the waves just beginning to show and the lush mountains of Tahiti filled the horizon. It was my watch and I noticed what I thought was a log afloat in a distant wave, but as we neared, a flash of flukes convinced me otherwise. We were headed for a collision and too close to alter course. I flipped on the depth sounder, hoping the high frequency waves would alert the 60-foot leviathan. He sounded yards from TR's port bow. I closed my eyes and held my breath. When I dared look, he surfaced just off our stern on the starboard side –whew! I would see many more whales over the years, but none that close.

In relative terms, Papeete is the big city: electronic cash registers, bumper to bumper traffic, hordes of people. There was no room on the town cay since most of the boats were now permanent residents so we anchored among several other transient yachts just off their bows. I thought it would be a case of nonstop musical boats until I realized the boats on the cay never went anywhere.

My first stop ashore was customs and immigration. The onslaught of destitute mariners and foreign tourists had initiated new rules for cruising permits. I now had to have a plane ticket that would guarantee my departure in case the boat sank. The paperwork was also a nightmare, but I hadn't been to Australia yet. I was able to book a one way flight to American Samoa with a local airline on my American Express card. This turned out to be a good move since the airline went belly-up a month later, but American Express still refunded the money.

The second stop was American Express to pick up mail. This was also a good move because the post office in Papeete held mail for only two weeks before it was returned. Mail, as you can imagine, is a really big deal for anyone who is traveling for long periods, and I met several cruisers who were absolutely heartbroken about missing their mail by a day or two. I found an outdoor cafe and sat under a fragrant frangipani tree to read my stack of letters. It was all reassuring news from home, including one from Linda who had made it safely back to Albuquerque and was now enrolled in nursing school. I'd done a pretty good job of keeping her out of my mind during the passage, but now she came barging in stirring up the sadness and regrets. I drank my coffee in a semi funk, staring off into the distance when someone slammed a large red bucket down on the table. I jerked back in surprise and Olivier said, "Here is your damn bucket!" – whoa. I suppose I deserved it but I had no idea he'd been so bitter and it really caught me off guard.

He told me he and Isabel would leave the boat and stay in Papeete to work. Originally they had planned to sail as far as New Caledonia where Olivier had an uncle, but after their experience in Columbia, they felt it necessary to work for a while and recoup the lost money. I think it had more to do with me and my priorities. Regardless, it was easier said than done since we learned they would need job sponsors before I could take them off TR's crew list. As captain, I was responsible for my crew and their passage out of French Polynesia.

That evening, as I sipped a cold beer at happy hour in a local bar, contemplating a single-handed trip to New Zealand, I met Claude and Jean Robert or JR as I came to call him.

Trolling for Sharks

The Fabled South Seas

"You always know when you've seen the real thing."

Papeete, like any big town, catered to consumerism and I wanted for nothing, even obscure engine parts for the Johnson outboard or bronze bearings for TR's windlass. The supermarkets like any in Florida. The French Navy was also accommodating and allowed a friend of mine to rebuild his boat's engine in their machine shop on the quay. But even paradise isn't exempt from the shabbier side of life. The day after our arrival, I was sitting in the cockpit watching the world go by when a rusty pickup truck screeched to a halt directly across the water from where TR was anchored. A large (think Sumo wrestler) Tahitian jumped from the driver's side, lumbered to the passenger side and yanked open the door. A young, slender woman tried to fend him off but he reached in, grabbed a fistful of her long black hair, dragged her, kicking, onto the sidewalk and proceeded to beat her with his other fist. Her screams fell on deaf ears. I felt helpless out on the water and was amazed that nobody tried to intervene as the abuse carried on for more than a minute. Sixty seconds can be a long damn time. The years I'd spent as a paramedic had hardened me to the results of these actions, but I never got used to the ugliness of the actual scene. When the woman finally collapsed in a heap, the guy threw her into the back of the truck and drove off – not exactly the welcome wagon.

It took about ten days to sort out my crew situation, but Olivier and Isabel both got jobs, she as an English teacher and he, as you would expect, a chef. Claude and JR had to finagle their way out of a six-month apartment lease, but ultimately pulled it off. My original plan with crew was to share expenses as we went along, but that got complicated as we changed currencies and someone would forget how much they spent for what. With Claude and JR, I decided to charge them each $10 per day and then I would pay for everything except visas or specialty items like booze and candy. This system would ultimately work the best for everyone. I didn't make money from the arrangement, but I didn't have to spend much of my own. As a result, when I got to places where TR needed extra work, the money was there.

In the interim I had the boat to myself which worked out well for me when I offered a dry bunk to a tall, angular, drowned looking Australian lady whose tent had been shredded in a fierce thunderstorm. When she finally dried out she was a striking woman. The first evening aboard we traded heartache stories then settled in to our respective bunks. Just before I nodded off for the night I heard a soft voice from the aft cabin ask, "Would you like company up there?" Yes, there is a God. The lady's name, if you can believe it, was Linda. We had a great few days together before she had to fly home for a waiting job. I found myself humming that old Beach Boys tune, "Help Me Rhonda."

Galley fare was bound to take a dive when Olivier departed, but I'm pretty handy in the kitchen and so were Claude and JR. I believe that a well fed crew is usually a happy crew and to this end I insisted whoever was cook for the day prepare one good meal be it breakfast, lunch or dinner. I also suggested that whoever cooked would also clean up. This didn't go over well with the two Frenchmen, so I cleaned my own messes and they worked it out amongst themselves. After a week of cleaning up after JR, Claude saw the light and understood why I chose to clean up after myself.

Sail magazine did an article on cruising yachts in the Pacific while I was in Polynesia and in an issue a few months later Theodora R was featured in a half page color photo under full sail, her tanbark sails set against the misty-green mountains of Moorea. She was impossible after that, demanding only the finest spar varnish. In Papeete I'd become friends with Jeff and Janelle, two Americans on the yacht Dark Star (they made the cover of that issue of Sail). We'd met in an empty stairwell, all of us in search of a mystery bar that was rumored to serve $1 beer at happy hour. Our paths would cross many times before reaching Australia. Like me, they too were keen for adventure.

An Australian film company was shooting "Mutiny On The

Bounty" in one of Moorea's more spectacular bays and we were fortunate enough to get the captain's tour of the Bounty replica. Even as a movie prop she was a very salty ship.

Moorea, like Tahiti was heavily touristic and after a long day on a moped to see the sights the crew and I opted for greener grass. It seemed Gaugin's Polynesia was nowhere to be found and I felt a little bit cheated. I laid a course for Huahine, 60 miles northwest.

On nautical charts the compass rose has a correction for magnetic variation and this must be added or subtracted to the compass course depending on whether or not the variation is east or west. There is a little rhyme that goes "West is best and east is least" to help with the choice of addition or subtraction. In one of my more dyslexic moments, I added instead of subtracted 15 degrees to our course (that made for a 30-degree error!) We upped anchor at 10 p.m. expecting to see the shores of Huahine at daybreak. It was a spirited reach with winds gusting to 30 knots and we ran with reefed main and staysail. Well, when the sun came up there was nothing but blue ocean as far as the eye could see. Definitely not the way to impress or instill confidence in new crew. My boys had suffered a touch of mal de mer on the lumpy ride, but to their credit showed high spirits despite the absence of a mountainous island. It didn't take long to spot my error and from my perch on TR's spreaders I located the wayward isle. I could only be thankful that there were no reefs on the course I'd taken. We were so far east of Huahine that, on the corrected course, it turned into a pleasant downwind sail. We dropped anchor at noon, the only boat in a quiet blue lagoon.

No resort hotel, no golf course, no discos. Two small inns and restaurant/bars of tastefully thatched design shared the beaches with nature. The proprietress of one bar was a lovely Polynesian/European mix whose heart and daughter belonged to a long departed French doctor. She played such extraordinary Tahitian rhythms on her guitar that after a few minutes of trying to imitate her right hand techniques on my own instrument, and failing, I sat back and just listened.

I took a couple of days to build a teak boom gallows for TR's heavy fir boom. Reefing the main in rolly seas had been a bit unruly because I had no way to secure the boom while shortening sail.

We cruised the inner lagoon for a few days to explore the more remote parts of Huahine, diving on abundant reefs and generally pigging out on seafood. Afterward, we sailed out the south pass and headed for Raitea. In Papeete I'd bought a set of post cards, each an aerial photo of the individual Society Islands. They clearly showed the entrances through the reefs, coral heads and shallows. I used these almost exclusively to navigate in and around the islands. Postcard in hand I found a narrow pass in the reef on the eastern side of Raitea. Just inside the lagoon a powerful squall put such a strain on TR's reefed main that a ½" retaining bolt snapped, resulting in a 3 foot tear in the sail. We found shelter at the back of a deep bay surrounded by unbroken thousand foot walls of tropical green. Dark Star was the only other boat there, and probably less than delighted to see TR intrude on their idyllic setting. Nevertheless, Jeff and Janelle came to my rescue with a stiff rum drink and a zigzag sewing machine.

A few days later we were tied to the copra jetty outside a fairly large village and were lucky enough to be invited to an island wide Tamare dance contest at the local high school that night. Over a hundred young women and men showed up in grass skirts, and sarongs ready to out-shake the competition. This was no tired dance troop from a resort hotel, this was pure nubile energy, heart and soul laid bare. Row after row of undulating hips kept time to a dozen drummers and wowed the crowd until after midnight. I'd never seen so much glistening flesh. You can always tell when you've seen the real thing.

In a flat calm we motored 6 hours to the fabled isle of Bora Bora, its distinctive volcanic core jutting into the blue. Claude and JR were looking forward to a wild time on Bastille Day, but celebration funds had been redirected to help out with El Nino relief throughout French Polynesia. Instead we had Rudy, a Swiss inventor who had devised some small valve for use in heart surgery and now joined his 60-foot motorsailor at exotic ports around the world. The crew's last port of call had been in Mexico where, with the peso recently devalued, they took on 120 cases of various booze. Lucky for us, their next stop would be Hawaii where the import duty on the liquor would be astronomical, so drastic measures were needed to reduce the inventory. Every evening at six, Rudy got on his loud hailer and announced "Open Bar," and dinghies from around the anchorage would converge on Rudy's boat for another all-hours party.

One vivid memory in an otherwise hazy recollection of Bora Bora, was anchoring in 90 feet of water, the deepest yet and a record that would hold for ten years. We attached an extra 150 feet of line to the chain just to get a minimal scope. Fortunately the wind never rose over 15 knots and I was delighted to have energetic crew to crank in all that chain when we left.

Mopelia, the western most atoll in French Polynesia, was a low coral island bristling with coconut palms and home to a village of 16 people. We arrived before dawn and even hove-to the current swept us past the island at four knots. It took two hours of motoring in flat seas to claw our way back two miles. I'd been told the entrance was quite narrow, but studded with coral heads too?! Rave reports on the diving here was the only thing that kept me from turning away. We anchored with two other yachts near the village. On rowing ashore, the chief and his wife (an amazing 350 lbs. each) welcomed us with bear hugs and fresh papaya. Tourism hadn't jaded this place. Wanting to reciprocate, we got together with the other cruisers and hosted a huge potluck meal for the locals. One of the boats had had their deep freeze fail and donated all the meat. The locals, not to be outdone, laid on an incredible luau two days later with suckling pig, roast chicken, hearts of palm salad, raw fish in lime and coconut milk, rice cooked in coconut milk and coconut pie for desert – no concern for weight loss here. This was the South Pacific dream and I felt as though I'd just experienced the tail end of a soon to be extinct phenomenon.

The diving, as promised, offered spectacular coral walls but the spear fishing was a bit dicey due to the ever-present black tip sharks. At one point, after spearing a parrot fish for dinner, a pack of about ten sharks started into a whirling frenzy not far from Claude and me. I signaled to Claude and we hightailed it to the dinghy fifty yards away. Just before we reached the dinghy, I looked back and saw two of the sharks break away and come straight for us. I jabbed my speargun into the face of one that took a fancy to Claude's fins. Claude was oblivious and laughed when I launched into the dinghy. Yeah, real funny!

The Chief took us out to a nearby motu riotous with nesting gannets. He marked off a ten-foot square and cleared the area of eggs. He would return in a few days and pick up any fresh eggs that were inside the square. We did the same and later sailed away with three dozen. Even knowing these folks more or less live off the land, I had a hard time watching them flip over a 400 lb. sea turtle and butcher it. But hey, it was their back yard. The next generation might do things differently.

Before we left, the chief suffered a nasty coral cut on one leg. The wound festered and the leg swelled to twice its normal size, (I mean HUGE). With the aid of a ham radio on one of the other yachts, we were able to report the situation to a doctor in Papeete via a radio patch through Hawaii. The next day a French destroyer showed up and took the chief back to Papeete for treatment. Three months later, we heard through the sailing grapevine that he returned on the copra boat in good health.

Christine was another indelible memory from Mopelia. She was a 90 lb., 65-year old, wiry Chinese/Tahitian mix who had asked us for aspirin because of chronic back pain. I'd assumed the back pain was just from old age, but found her one morning lugging 120 lb. sacks of fresh copra two hundred yards to the drying racks. She made an impressive sight, this little stick of a woman with a monster load on her shoulder. I left her a whole bottle of aspirin.

I never met a cruiser in the tropics that didn't have an issue with cockroaches. It seems the buggers are unavoidable. There is a saying, that if you see one cockroach there are hundreds more in hiding. Well, by the time we reached Mopelia we were seeing more than one, but at least they were the small variety. I donned my scuba gear and armed myself with three large cans of bug killer, all different brands and sprayed the devil out of every possible hidey-hole. We closed up the boat and returned after many hours. The carpet on the cabin sole couldn't be seen through the blanket of dead roach bodies.

Mopelia was one of those places where you could find yourself five years later wondering where the time went. But we finally managed to pull ourselves away, intrigued by Suvarov atoll, the northern-most possession of the Cook Islands. Little did I know the pain and aggravation that was headed my way.

Fitful winds drew the 500-mile passage out to six days and for a while I'd abandoned Suvarov due to direct headwinds. These winds eventually shifted but left a nasty cross-sea. In a careless moment stepping into the cockpit TR lurched and I was thrown into the spoked wheel. A loud pop and sharp pain told me I'd fractured a rib. In New Zealand I would fit a stainless steel band around the wheel to cover the spokes and install a safety bar on the console so I would have something to hang onto in the middle of the cockpit.

Suvarov is a twenty-mile long ring of coral with several motus five hundred miles from anywhere and is the quintessential deserted tropical paradise − plenty of resources and no mosquitoes. On an island no more than an acre square, Tom Neale, a Kiwi hermit had made his home for several years before a back injury forced him out. He wrote a book about his experiences entitled An Island of my Own. Tom's bungalow and a WWII spotting tower were still maintained by visiting cruisers. Cook Island fisherman would occasionally make the trip for a guaranteed bountiful catch. Spearfishing, however, was a one shot affair. The sound of a spear gun going off brought a posse of sharks so your first shot had to count. Once, when shadowed by a five-foot reef shark, I thrust my spear gun into his face to scare him off, but he promptly bit down on the business end of the gun. I was sorely tempted to pull the trigger, but figured I would lose at least the spear. I yanked the gun free and abandoned the hunt.

Dark Star arrived a couple of days after us and we mounted an expedition to a wrecked freighter several miles along the reef. We crossed the half-mile of reef at low tide in a foot of water. About halfway there, our sloshing feet attracted small black tip sharks. These were potentially lethal, our ankles being bite-sized morsels. We grabbed up loose chunks of coral and kept watch in all four directions. I'd yell "Incoming at three o'clock," and we'd hurl our missiles at the approaching fin. In this manner we made it safely there and back. The wreck, an old Korean rust bucket, was no great shakes and definitely not worth the risk. But then, you never know when you'll find that hidden treasure.

The anchorage was deep and full of coral heads and the anchor chain would frequently come up short when it wrapped around one of the heads. I found an old 400-lb. fluke anchor near the reef and decided it would make a great mooring. We eased TR over the anchor at high tide, lifted it just off the sand with the windlass and moved it to deep water. When we dropped it, it landed precariously across a coral head. My idea was to just dive down and push it off. Our activities had roused the curiosity of several large black tip sharks, but we were used to them by now and they posed no threat. Claude and I dove down twenty feet and gave the anchor a shove. It tilted and toppled off the coral. Unfortunately the anchor's shank bounced against the coral where I'd placed my hand. Claude said I screamed underwater, but I don't remember. I do remember swimming fast for the surface. My nearly severed middle finger dangled from my hand and gushing blood turned the water green. All I could think about were the sharks.

Once we'd scrambled up the boarding ladder, I managed to put my brain on hold and got down to the business of treating the hand. Through my medical connections as a paramedic, TR carried a substantial first aid kit. There was plenty of injectable xylocain to numb the finger for a thorough cleaning. Infection was my biggest worry. It took two hours and thirty stitches to sew the digit back on, me sewing and Claude tying the knots. Pain arrived the next day. My crew and the folks on Dark Star did their best to make things easy for me, but I was one cranky SOB.

I was ready to roll in five days and roll we did. With two plastic bags taped over the bandaged hand and plenty of aspirin, we set sail for Tonga. Fortified tradewinds had blown for weeks and the waves were a good eight to ten feet. TR raced along at six knots on a beam reach under reefed main only for five days on what was definitely my worst sailing experience thus far. The decks were constantly awash in green water and every now and then a wave would even break into the mainsail, filling the cockpit. Bill was useless in these conditions so we hand-steered the entire time − two on and four off. Within twenty-four hours we felt like numb robots. I had a hell of a time keeping my hand dry especially when using the sextant. The trip wasn't all that great for my crew either. JR was seasick most of the time and Claude got stuck with all the cooking. I recall our immense relief when we sailed into the lee of the Vava'u Group in northern Tonga on a sunny, quiet Sunday morning.

Flat batteries forced us to sail five miles upwind through narrow, winding channels between the islands to the anchorage at Neifu. But we were warm and dry and actually enjoyed the work. I was really proud of my crew when we tacked flawlessly through the last dogleg, wove through twenty anchored yachts and laid TR gently alongside the customs jetty.

After that last passage, the next five weeks were an extreme high. Nowhere have I experienced such immediate acceptance into a local community – they don't call them the "Friendly Islands" for nothing. When we cleared in we were given a pamphlet of basic Tongan phrases and guide to their social culture – isn't that clever.

The "almost a doctor" at the clinic took an x-ray of my finger; helped me remove the stitches, and invited us to a wedding feast – terrific bedside manner. The x-ray showed a dislocation at the first joint, but a quick jerk on the finger fixed that. Although it's a tad crooked, I now have full use of the finger.

At the wedding feast all the guests were served first by attending relatives. Pork, seafood, vegetables and fruit had all been drenched in coconut milk and wrapped in taro leaves the day before then placed in layers in a pit. The pit was filled with sand and a bonfire built on top as taught in luau 101. When every guest had eaten his or her fill, we were all excused and sent on our way so the rels could finish up the extensive remains. No tedious after-dinner chitchat at these get togethers, eliminating the need to be nice to folks you might not like.

Being a nut for textiles, I was in my element. Tongan baskets are some of the finest in the world and after TR absorbed all she could handle, I sent quite a few to my sister in New Mexico. I was also introduced to the making of tapa cloth, which is pounded mulberry bark held together with a paste made from the cassava root. Thin sheets of bark are layered with a mallet into large sheets of fabric, up to 120sq. ft. Once dried, the fabric is painted and cut up for clothes, bedding and, in these days, decorative wall hangings. One day I'd hiked several miles along a seldom-used road into the bush. I began hearing a rhythmic drumming off in the distance, dada deda – dada deda – dada deda. Intrigued, I followed my ears to the source. Sitting under a wide shade tree were three women pounding out sheets of tapa. They each sat in front of a separate beam of hardwood sprung on both ends with smaller sticks. With one hand they pulled pasted strips of mulberry bark from a large dish and with the other kept a continuous pounding rhythm with their mallet all in a groove with the other two. The sheets of tapa grew and grew to their drumming and I'm not even sure they were ever aware that I was there.

With only 73 shopping days left before Christmas, I packed up a hand-woven clothes hamper with local crafts and sent it to the states. It arrived in great shape in less than thirty days.

A couple of weeks into our stay, I met a woman (and I'm not kidding, her name was Linda) from California who'd jumped ship. She'd signed on as cook and all was well until Tonga, where the owner decided to leave after three days. Linda, having come so far and seen so little, was having none of it and decided to stay. After a tentative courtship of three or four hours, she signed on as my new first mate and companion. JR and Claude loved her cooking. She had long black hair, a perfect American smile and her bikinis made a nice departure from our locker-room dress. We cruised the out islands of northern Tonga for three weeks to make sure of the arrangement and galley fare rose to new heights. However, we did discover that Vaselined gannet eggs do not last as long as chicken eggs. JR had decided to bake a cake while Linda and I lounged in the cockpit. That distinct foul odor of rotten eggs wafted from below followed directly by a pale JR who lunged pitifully into the cockpit before all thought of cake erupted from clenched teeth. I was supremely happy that the discovery wasn't made during a passage.

The local elixir, made from ground kava root and mixed with water to a thin mud consistency, produced a mild lethargic high. As far as I could discern its consumption was limited to the men and was usually accompanied by a ceremonious clapping of hands, which did nothing to improve the flavor – sugar doesn't help either. All in all, not unlike meeting your buddies at the local bar for a brew.

Glass jars and cotton bed sheets were high value trade items and TR left Tonga a little threadbare but we collected some great Tapa and carved coral. Besides, new linen was only a week away in Fiji.

Our planned departure from Fiji was delayed a few days due to strong headwinds, but when we did sail out the pass, a pod of twenty pilot whales escorted us for the first few miles. I took this as a good omen, which was soon canceled out by the BBC broadcast of the last race of the 1983 America's Cup when the cup left America for the first time in the history of the race. I spent most of the passage writing an article about the mishap in Suvarov and sent it to Cruising World. Months later, they bought and published it, which took some of the pain out of the experience.

The Fiji Islands are also bound by extensive coral reefs and I chose to heave-to at midnight when we were ten miles out, negotiating the long narrow entrance into Suva at dawn. We anchored in the quarantine zone, but since it was Sunday TR conveniently suffered engine problems that delayed our arrival at the customs dock by a day and saved us the overtime charges. These charges varied from twenty to a hundred dollars depending on the place, so tactics like mechanical trouble saved a tidy sum over the years.

After Papeete, Suva was a real bargain for everything from marine hardware to food. After two months of a laid-back cruising environment the place felt frantic. The Suva yacht club was a colonial throwback that graciously offered peaceful solace from the madness of town. But if you were caught wearing a hat in the bar it would cost you a round. Over thirty cruising boats swung at anchor in the bay, most of the yachties taking advantage of the club's facilities, delighted at the prospect of a washing machine. Claude and JR kept their own schedules. There was plenty of dinghy traffic around the anchorage so rides ashore or back out weren't a problem. I only asked, if they returned quite late, to keep the noise down and we all got along fine.

Linda and I became addicted to the sights and smells of the Suva spice market, where East Indian vendors hawked their wares. Even if we weren't shopping for anything in particular, we'd always come away with at least one carefully wrapped sack of something to brighten up dinner or dispel bilge odors. Before we left Suva our favorite vendor, a petit Indian woman swathed in a red and gold sari, mixed us a special blend of curry for TR's spice shelf. I've never found one to replace it.

My friends on Dark Star almost lost their boat on the reef. An inexperienced crewmember had been on watch the night they arrived and hove-to in an almost dead calm off the entrance. A swift onshore current swept Dark Star onto the reef and was hard aground before evasive action could be taken. The reef was two miles wide at that point, but a salvage company using a long hawser attached to a small tug dragged the boat safely across the entire distance. Dark Star came through with only superficial hull damage. Egos and pocketbooks took the real beating.

On a hitchhiking excursion inland, a middle-aged Fijian in a battered truck picked up Linda and me. He hastily made room for us in the cab. I was taken aback by the sight of thousands of dollars in cash, rubber-banded together in tight bundles and piled on the dash. He was on his way to a distant lumber mill with the payroll, and I couldn't help wondering about his trusting nature and whether it was a good thing or not.

Like us, many of the yachts in Suva were headed to New Zealand for the hurricane season. The Kiwis required a visa prior to entering the country, but in order to qualify for a visa each boat had to show financial solvency to the order of $4000.00. Nobody that I knew carried that much cash aboard so a number of us pooled our resources and came up with a bundle of money that we took turns using when applying for our visas. If the folks at the Kiwi consulate noticed anything similar to everybody's hoard of cash, they didn't say anything.

After a couple weeks of big city living, we cruised eastward to the out-islands where "The finest diving in the South Pacific" was to be found. On the island of Yanutha, legendary home of firewalkers, I met a six-toed firewalker who invited me, Claude and JR to a local kava ceremony. Thinking this may ultimately lead to witnessing a trance-like stroll through burning embers, I willingly partook, leaving aboard a miffed first mate. But alas, the firewalking ritual only took place at the resort hotels on the mainland. At our new friend's insistence we attended the show at the Sheraton one night and watched him hop from hot rock to hot rock, in a less than spectacular event that anyone with well-callused feet could imitate.

On our approach to the lower end of the Yasawa group, we were caught amongst a labyrinth of reefs by a severe thunderstorm. The rain felt like sand particles and stung the skin. After quickly dropping sail, we donned jackets, masks and snorkels in order to see and breathe then motored slowly forward keeping the reef ten feet to port. An exhausting hour later we safely entered the lagoon. The diving did prove outstanding, but the reefs had been pretty well fished out, leaving lots of small, psychedelic tropical fish swarming the coral. I did manage to snag two large lobsters, the first since the Caribbean. Dividing the spoils amongst the crew was easy. Claude and JR preferred the green slimy stuff inside the heads, leaving the tails to Linda and me. Sometimes I had to wonder about the French appetite. This convenient division of food worked well with cheese too. After opening a vacuum packed chunk of cheddar, it would begin to spoil after a week. That is when Claude and JR chose to eat it and I would open a fresh packet for Linda and me.

In the two weeks of cruising the relatively uninhabited Yasawas most of our socializing was among other cruisers. On one island where there were three other yachts besides TR, Linda declared a haircutting day. She gave 14 haircuts over the afternoon including whacking off a good six inches of JR's bushy dome. Three weeks later, he would rue the loss on the frosty mornings.

We set sail for Kiwiland to hide from hurricanes on November 13th with light easterlies, air temp in the eighties. The four-person crew reduced watch time considerably to two hours on and six hours off, making the 1100-mile trip sound like a vacation. Until now I'd been sailing what is known as the "milk run" or within 30 degrees of the equator where other than hurricanes, which are usually seasonal, there is no dangerously bad weather. Things may get a bit uncomfortable from time to time but not life-threatening. The north end of New Zealand is in the high thirties of latitude and the snake coiled into a tight ball. We wouldn't be near 30 degrees south for at least a week but that snake wouldn't relax. As if foreshadowing disaster, the wind shifted to a brisk southwester the first afternoon and by morning we were 100 miles to the east of our rhumbline course. My birthday dawned and the wind backed to the south. I promptly smashed my knee on the companionway entrance and doubled its size. Linda, bless her, braved lumpy seas in the galley and cranked out a terrific chocolate layer cake which almost made me forget about the knee. Just before sundown two seventy-foot, sperm whales spouted a hundred yards upwind from the boat. Moments later, the low-tide aroma of whale breath washed over us. Yes, that was quite a fine birthday present.

The wind teased us for another ten days before filling in from the east. Our progress until then had been frustratingly erratic but the weather had spared us any discomfort – shorts and T-shirts all the way. Two days out of Whangerei, our intended port of call, air temp dropped thirty degrees. The next morning we could see our breath. From the bowels of the ship we scrounged for any clothing of substance then wrapped ourselves in blankets to stand watch. A pot of hot soup simmered continuously on the stove. Thanksgiving dinner started with creamed spinach and mushroom soup followed by makeshift lasagna of cheddar cheese, breadcrumbs, pepperoni and tomato sauce, topped off with prune pie. And yes, we were running short on a few stores.

Earthy smells engulfed us as we motored against light headwinds into the Bay of Islands on an aquamarine sea. Rolling hills thick with evergreens layered away in the distance. A fine mist hung over the headlands and other than the lighthouse, there was no sign of civilization. The meat-hook line snapped taut and we landed a 10-pound tuna for our celebration feast. New Zealand officials must have gotten wind of the cheap pot in Panama, because they had the dogs on hand to meet arriving yachts. I'd made sure we left Tahiti drug free just for this reason.

Claude and JR were on the road via bicycle within days. I wished them well on their future travels and hope to see them in France one day. Linda would stay on as first mate and traveling companion until a better offer came along. My friend, R.B. White, from Albuquerque arrived a week later for a short visit on his way to Sydney. With my friends from Dark Star and several other yachties we hiked into the bush on a wild goat safari and brought back barbecue fixings for the entire fleet of this year's cruising crowd anchored at Whangerei. With no shortage of fresh dairy products, and Linda's cooking, R.B left us a few pounds heavier.

The NZ dollar had recently devalued giving my U.S. dollars a 50% hedge on the cost of living and boat maintenance. The Pacific crossing hadn't been easy on TR and she begged for a serious refit. This would be the ideal place to oblige the old girl.

Native canoe

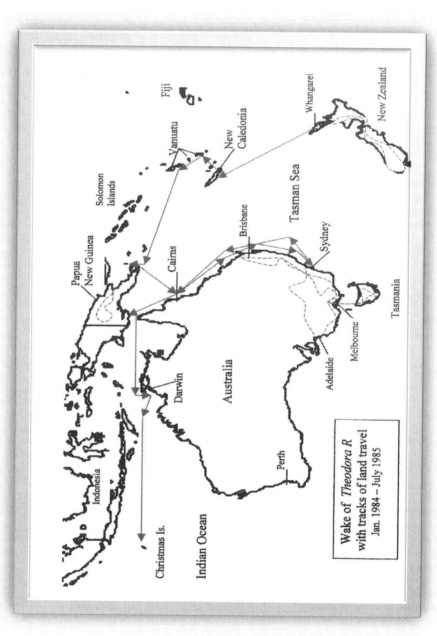

Wake of *Theodora R*
with tracks of land travel
Jan. 1984 – July 1985

New Zealand and Beyond

"After a while, you just get used to it."

I'd been afloat for two years and I have to say, it was a relief to be off the water for a while. Not that there was anything romantic about living on a boat propped up high and dry in a noisy boatyard, but I didn't miss those midnight anchor drills and rolly anchorages. For the next three and a half months TR would get her refit and then some. With the US dollar so strong, I would be able to go beyond the necessities. Linda took on the job of burning off all the old bottom paint, which in some places was a quarter inch thick and had begun peeling off in Fiji. She also did a fine job of keeping us fed. Her participation allowed me to put in a straight 8-10 hours everyday on TR's upgrades. These consisted of new stainless steel rigging, stripping and repainting the hull, new electrical system, additional fastenings around the mast step (the area where the mast sits on the keel), new caulking in some weepy seams, repairing and replacing sails, a custom spray dodger, rebuilding the rudder and addressing countless minor deficiencies. The most tedious project though was replacing the wooden bulwarks – an 8" high rail around her decks.

Before TR was craned from the water, my mom, her husband Jack and my brother Chris came for a visit over the holidays. The lot of us got a taste of what life aboard one of the King's ships must have been like. If one of us turned without caution, beware an elbow in the eye.

We rented a car and spent a week touring the central part of the North Island. Jack and I chartered a boat in the lake country and landed several huge rainbow trout.

It's doubtful whether Connie and Jack would ever have come to these lands down-under if it wasn't for me. I was definitely their excuse for travel and each year they would appear at some corner of the world where TR swung at anchor. Their visits worked out great, forcing me off the boat to participate in a lot of touristy things I would otherwise blow off for either lack of interest or funds. They were both quite adventurous, game for exploration of all sorts except those that were too physically taxing. For long hikes, serious diving or mountain climbing I was on my own.

The boatyard where TR would dry her bones for over two months was only a short walk from the center of town allowing general access to the community. But what I found out here was that if you weren't part of the workforce (foreigners working on their own boats didn't count) getting in tight with the locals was near impossible. At these times I almost regretted having the income to avoid work. Even though in most cases it was illegal to work anywhere as a foreigner without a permit, many cruisers, out of necessity, would seek general labor jobs to build next year's cruising kitty. From the jobs came the invitations into the more intimate side of the community, family cookouts and that type of thing, where one can get an insight into the true world-view of the average citizen. But TR kept me plenty busy and I rarely had the time or desire to stop in at the local pub for a brew after a day's work.

The wooden bulwarks required a lot of specialized milling of parts. I was directed to a small lumberyard where I found just the wood I needed. The yard also had a complete shop full of industrial woodworking equipment. I handed the foreman a drawing with all the detailed specs for the cuts. He told me he was too busy to take on the project, but before I dropped to my knees to beg, he said if I knew how to run the equipment I was free to use their shop – HUH? Having recently come from the land of contingency law practice, and astronomical liability insurance, I was shocked by the offer. Of course I took him up on it and came to realize that the Kiwis took responsibility for themselves and would never consider asking someone else to pay for their own stupidity or clumsiness. I later found this to be true in Australia and South Africa as well. What happened to America?

As a whole I found New Zealanders complacently content and not overly ambitious. Example - One of the best stainless steel propane marine stoves on the market was manufactured in

Auckland. A friend of mine had one installed in a new boat he'd commissioned at the yard where TR was hauled. When he began using the stove, he found the burner adjustment had no low setting and it was almost impossible to get a low flame without extinguishing the flame. He called the owner of the company, explained the problem and the guy says, "I have the same stove in my own boat and after a while you just get used to it." The propane stove in TR's galley is a low priced enameled model but even those burner valves have an automatic low setting. This was only one example of a prevailing attitude that, if nothing else, went a long way toward reducing stress.

As work on TR neared completion, Linda got an offer to help deliver a new yacht from Finland to San Francisco. It was an offer impossible to refuse and she flew back to the states with a declaration to meet up with me in Sydney. I would miss her but at the same time I wasn't despondent. We hadn't been together all that long and TR's demands would see that I wasn't too lonely. I splashed on the last dab of bottom paint and made plans for a well-earned trip to the South Island. When the crane set TR back in the water, I was surprised to find she had lost 1500 pounds − over 150 gallons of water − from her hull through evaporation. Just when I thought I'd tended to TR's every whim, she developed an evil knock in her engine that only a new set of rod bearings would satisfy. That was two days of messy, finger-mashing work that, luckily, I was able to perform in situ.

Hitchhiking in New Zealand proved very efficient. I was even given rides by old ladies and young girls and wholesome families. Sometimes they invited home for dinner and a spare bed. Apparently there was a lack of serial killers on the loose. I carried a marker pen and sheets of cardboard and would write out my destination. If I didn't get a ride right away, I would turn the sign upside down. Invariably the next motorist, out of an innate sense of politeness, would stop to correct my mistake. If for some reason that ploy didn't work, I would hold up the sign from the place I just came from with the same well-meaning results. I rarely waited more than twenty minutes for a ride.

Wellington reminded me of a mini San Francisco with its early architecture, steep hills and picturesque bay. It was nothing for me to spend all day just walking, whether in cities or the country, probably as a counterbalance to sitting on the boat. I also noticed a lot more at that pace. Even on a bicycle, scenes seemed to fly past, a blur of color, little impression. After two days in a place like Wellington, I knew my way around better than most people who had lived there for a year.

I rode the ferry across Cook straight and hitched over to Nelson to renew an old acquaintance from my Albuquerque days. Adrian Studer, tall and slender with dark features and the air of a stern schoolmaster, was an accomplished violinmaker and had set up shop in Nelson. He and his wife June made me feel at home even after I chopped some onions on her breadboard. Adrian had just finished a new shop building and I was able to help build in benches and shelving. The whole scene, wood-chips on the floor, the smell of newly planed spruce and ebony, musicians stopping by, twanged my heartstrings and for the first time since leaving New Mexico I was adrift on a wave of nostalgia. When I'd told my friends I was selling out and going sailing some were amazed that I could "Throw it all away." "You've got it made," they said. And in terms of the American dream, I did, but life was a bit dull, no extreme highs and lows to accent one another. Sailing certainly provided that and until now I hadn't given my past life a thought. But after a few days I recognized the routine and got over it.

For a small town, Nelson was uniquely cosmopolitan, with a significant cross section of Europeans in residence. Food co-ops were a mainstay and Nelson is the only place in the world I ever found bacon flavored TVP (textured vegetable protein) in bulk. I hauled 5lbs. of it back to the boat with me. Due to some topographical oddity, Nelson enjoyed relatively mild and sunny weather which I'm sure wasn't lost on anybody living there. I could easily see myself taking up residence, but I think a visa would be a problem.

Sailing connections put me in touch with the owner of a large sheep station on the South Island. I spent a couple days tramping about the mountains with a pack of incredible sheep dogs. I've never been more impressed with animals that so totally knew their business. With a few subtle hand-signs and the odd whistle, six dogs had complete control over a thousand sheep. Unlike the U.S., where disease and predators take a serious toll on livestock, Kiwis can pretty well count on taking the whole herd to market and it's a thriving business. For this reason, animals on cruising boats are frowned upon. People aboard get six-month visas, animals two weeks and then they aren't allowed off the boat. As you can imagine, the Kiwis are very strict about this and violators lose their animals.

I crossed paths with some sailing buddies that were picking apples to boost the cruising kitty. We trekked around two of the national parks in the area where hiking was quite civilized with well-groomed trails, overnight cabins furnished with bunks, stoves, water and free pre-chopped firewood.

After I'd been on the road for about six weeks, I bought a two-week rail pass that entitled me to unlimited bus, train and ferry rides and gave me access to the rest of the South Island. In Fiordland my arrival at Milford sound coincided with the first snowfall. Hundreds of waterfalls poured from the thousand-foot cliffs rising from the sea turning the entire sound into one huge spectacular fountain shot through with rainbows.

I bussed up to the Tasman and Franz Joseph Glaciers and down to Invercargill at the very southern tip, then hit Dunedin and Christchurch on the way back up. Funny, nobody on a bus ever invited me home for a meal. The cold weather hurried me along and my cursory sightseeing didn't do any of those places justice, but I wanted an impression, since I didn't think I'd ever make it back. Several things stuck in my mind. I never saw any homeless or desperately poor people, all the horses looked healthy and the only thing that got a Kiwi's feathers up was nuclear energy.

Back in Whangerei I began looking for crew in earnest. I wanted someone who would make the entire season's trip to Sydney, because I knew changing crew in the islands would be a hassle, although I was prepared to singlehand it. Of a dozen applicants, only one wanted to make the whole trip. Lucia hailed from Switzerland and was out to see the world. She was in her twenties, short and dark with a cherubic face. She seemed gung-ho and thankfully traveled light. We spent a week cruising the Bay of Islands as a shakedown and compatibility test. Neither of us was interested in a relationship, which made everything easier. Adrian and June drove up to say goodbye and brought me the old Singer 306-k zigzag sewing machine I'd bought in Nelson. The machine I had wasn't up to the job, but this Singer should really eat the dacron.

My friends on Dark Star, Jeff and Janelle, had been "on the hard" next to TR in the boatyard repairing the hull damage suffered in Fiji, plus attending to numerous other changes that all us cruisers seem inclined to do. When I returned from my tour south, it was abundantly clear that Janelle would soon be a mother. Their son would be born in New Zealand a few months later while I was somewhere in New Guinea.

We sailed for New Caledonia a thousand miles to the north with a fair wind from the south. Three hundred pleasurable miles ticked by and gave Lucia a chance to get her sea legs. Early on the fourth day, a full gale pounced from the southwest pushing winds to 50 knots. Seas grew to 18 feet and TR's new rigging hummed a high G#. Bill hung in valiantly and steered for two days allowing us to spend much of the time below decks where everything felt deceptively calm. On one smoking wave I heard Bill's rudder snap in half and for the next four days we steered by hand. The wind soon moderated to a steady 25 knots and the sea lost its menace. Lucia took it all in stride and even attempted to cook a few meals. She appeared nonplussed over the sea conditions and Bill's demise, so I was surprised when a day out from Noumea she informed me she would be leaving the boat there. If we'd had a disagreement of some kind I could have understood, but we hadn't and I was really put out. I could only surmise she had planned this all along. She told me that traveling by boat wasn't what she thought it would be.

What I'd planned as a three day stop turned into two weeks tied stern-to at the Noumea yacht club with a crew wanted sign hung from the boomkin. But life was far from dull. The hard drinking Aussies were on the loose for a season's cruise with no distinction between night and day. Their revelry made sleep a rare commodity and I wore out the strings on my guitar. I also vented my frustration with recent crew by writing an article about taking on crew, the plusses and pitfalls, which was later published in Australia Sailing who paid 10 cents per word - writing is no way to make ends meet.

I had come there specifically to buy more of the plastic shoes I'd found in the Caribbean. One shop in town carried a large supply and I bought all their size 10's (8 pair) which I figured would last me until I reached the next French outpost. I also discovered a wine shop with a terrific selection of reds at less than $4 a bottle. I was amazed at how many of those bottles would fit in TR's bilge.

I met Dave, a tall blonde Englishman who looked a lot like John Denver, a week into my stay. He'd been programming government computers for several months and was looking for a break in his routine. He was an ardent smoker and it took him a week to decide if he could refrain from smoking on board. In the interim we banged round town, hitting the odd nightclub, but not only were these expensive, most had stringent dress codes that my wardrobe on TR couldn't possibly satisfy. I don't believe I ever met a cruiser with a pair of lace-up dress shoes aboard. I opined that the French here took the vanity thing to bizarre heights. But their fashion consciousness saved me a bundle.

Dave was the first crewmember I'd had aboard who actually had a fair amount of sailing experience. This isn't necessarily a good thing. With green crew, the skipper can train them to do things like coil lines or tie off cleats in the manner the skipper prefers. With someone like Dave (who had a contrary streak in him anyway) the matter seemed always up for debate. By the time we got to Sydney I would literally shudder when he would begin a sentence with, "Mind you...".

Our first stop leaving Noumea was the Isle of Pines, so named for the expansive grove of Norfolk Pines covering the island, a truly surreal sight after all the palm trees. The coral and sea-life here were outstanding and the two hundred or so residents maintained a healthy agro business. Fresh baguettes were available daily from the local bakery. We were the only boat anchored in a deep crescent bay. For a quiet, comfortable getaway place I rated it a 10. I went reefwalking with a local family during low tide to gather shellfish and octopus. The women waded through tidepools wielding machetes and sliced into schools of squid trapped in the pools – a unique fishing experience.

A day's sail north we overnighted at Ouvea atoll where 21 churches fought for the souls of the 240 inhabitants. When they came for mine we pressed on to Port Vila, Vanuatu on the Island of Efate. During the light-wind passage, I was below when I heard what I thought was rain. When I climbed topside into a cloudless sky, TR was plowing her way through an immense field of pumice evidently thrown up by a recent underwater eruption. The small brown pellets rattled along the waterline for a day and a half. Over the next few months, these pellets would eventually saturate and hang in suspension enticing local fish populations to gobble them up. The glasslike consistency of the pumice would ulcerate the fish intestines to a deadly outcome, interrupting a vital food chain and leading to an unprecedented number of fatal shark attacks in the region, one of which I would soon witness.

Vanuatu (ex New Hebrides) was in the midst of their third independence celebration when TR's anchor plowed the sand in Port Vila. We rowed ashore for a cursory check with customs, received colorful stamps in our passports then headed for the parade grounds. A pulsating throng of painted tribesmen with two-foot dangling penis sheathes held center stage. They each brandished a long wooden phallus and plunged them rhythmically into the earth with a chanted "Hoooga, Hoooga." This group had successfully eluded the missionaries.

A rectangle of food booths bordered the fairground serving all manner of protein and starch. Half a dozen of these touted high potency kava root that guaranteed a zippy high and I thought it made sense to let the drug dealers add to the GNP instead of locking them up.

Since obtaining independence from the shared French and English imperialization offshore banking was the up and coming industry. The beef business also flourished and I could buy grade-A cuts for under $2 per pound. I bought twenty pounds, had the butcher slice it super thin and made my own brand of jerky. Later I would do the same with some of the large tuna and mackerel caught during a long passage.

The harbor was so flat and calm that Dave and I took the opportunity to repaint TR's topsides the color of rich cream. It was something I had planned to do in New Zealand, but after three months of boat work I ran out of fortitude. It took us two weeks of sporadic work and TR looked like a new boat when we'd finished. Cosmetically I always tried to maintain what I call the thirty-foot look – at thirty feet she looked great. I never had the patience or desire for the five-foot look and my favorite color was the mossy green of tarnished bronze.

At the Vila Club, an integrated colonial stronghold, Dave introduced me to the game of snooker. As a pool player, I was way out of my league. There is no such thing as a slop shot in snooker. One of the few things Dave and I actually agreed on was that it would take serious refinement for a pool player to shoot a tight game of snooker. By the time we left Vila, Dave was known around the anchorage as "Argumentative Dave", which gave me an indication that I wasn't the only one with whom Dave played devil's advocate.

On the island of Epi, we met a couple of English expats trying to mechanize the local fishing industry. The Japanese had donated dozens of outboard motors, which were then mounted to the sailing canoes. And yes, they caught more fish since they had access to wider fishing grounds, but all the profits and more were going to Shell Oil and the Yamaha parts department and not enriching the local economy. It was a classic example of technology creating a lose-win situation.

TR, in the company of two other yachts, sailed to a nearby volcano, 5000 ft. of cinder cone jutting alone from the water. After cruising what I called terminally green islands, the stark barren moonscape in grayscale brought relief to my eyes. We anchored in the lee and attempted an assault on the summit. Half way up, dodging steam jets and fissures belching gaseous rotten eggs, we turned back when my shoes began to melt.

After several days of rolly, open roadstead anchorages we were looking for someplace calm. The island of Malekula offered several fine hidey-holes and a promise of fresh fruit. In the company of two other boats, we found Port Sandwich, a deep circular bay inside a fishhook headland. Early the next morning we set off in search of a rumored bakery and market. A five-mile, hot dusty walk yielded a sack of yams. On return to the boats, several of us took the plunge. A youngster and his friend were diving off their dinghy and I was scrubbing scum from TR's waterline when behind me I heard an odd swooshing sound followed by a piercing scream. Somehow I knew even before I spun around what had happened. The young boy and the shark were never seen again. A moment of hysteria while everyone vaulted from the water was followed by a helpless, disturbing silence that seemed louder than any sound I'd ever heard. For all of us there, paradise had lost its appeal.

Chased by ghosts and an ugly memory, Dave and I moved quickly up the island chain to Santo, where we reprovisioned and set sail for Papua, New Guinea. The 1100 miles of classic tradewind sailing helped restore our psyche. Other than a near collision with a small freighter late one night, the passage gurgled peacefully by with Bill on a 24/7 watch. I put a serious dent in a stack of mindless novels and honed my navigational skills using the volume of Selected Stars. Dave argued chess with Bobby Fisher. The meat hook kept us in fresh tuna or mackerel almost daily and there were moments when I thought sailing was a terrific way to travel.

New Guinea and the Great Barrier Reef

"Where are your guns?"

Until now, my image of New Guinea had been a jungle scene with some Rockefellian adventurer simmering in a giant black pot. Over the next month I would experience a few rough spots from sporting events to the treacherous volcanic landscape where near vertical terrain smothered in sweltering rain forest defied modern attempts at development. In some cases my original view seemed tame.

Dave and I stopped briefly in the out islands to clear customs then sailed into the bight of Milne bay on the east coast and dropped anchor in the busy little port of Alotau. As the hub for all the inter-bay traffic, small private vessels loaded with people and produce putted in and out at all hours. The teardrop shaped bay was lined with coconut palms and as was the custom, we tied TR's stern to a vacant tree. In the open market, we struck up a friendship with Tony, one of the local high school teachers. He invited us to join him on a "short" trek over the peninsula that afternoon to meet a group of students visiting from Australia and guide them back. Dave and I were both game and hopped into the back of his truck with our guide, 14-year-old Isaac, whose family lived at trails end. We drove for an hour to the trailhead, crossing five lively riverbeds along the way. We bogged down in the last, but a group of women doing laundry helped push us from the soft gravel. Since it was the dry season we were confident of an easy stroll but the first hundred yards of sludgy mud that repeatedly sucked the sandals off my feet gave evidence to the contrary. Our guide moved with alacrity through the root choked forest hopping nimbly from rock to rock and branch to rock (I think he'd done this before) while the rest of us floundered up the invisible trail. It took us three hours to travel four miles crossing the river 32 times before we reached the village only to find our reason for going, not there. We started back with 2 hours of daylight left, but a sudden torrential rain raised the river level almost 6 feet. We called a halt after Tony lost his footing and, had we not been linking arms, would have been swept away in the roiling torrent. Figuring we were stuck for the night, we fashioned a hasty shelter from available ground cover and waited out the rain. Just before dark the waters receded and our guide brought us to his folk's grass hut that under the circumstances could have passed for the Hilton. A gracious hostess fed us a hot meal of yams, rice and fish (standard village fare) and provided us with sleeping mats in a private corner of the hut. I remember one wall decorated with pages torn from an Australian magazine. They were all full-page color ads for major appliances, the beaming white faces of middle class housewives smiling at an inside joke.

The return trip went without hitch and we were back at the boat long enough to rest up for the night's big show at the school auditorium in honor of the visiting Aussies who had arrived by boat. Tony had mentioned something about a traditional yam harvest dance. Being in high school once myself I had a notion of what to expect.

Lights dimmed, drums thumped a slow beat as a snaking procession of oiled, full-breasted nubile girls dressed only in short grass tutus pulsated across the stage. The beat quickened and a matching number of strapping young lads appeared in loincloths brandishing giant phallic yams (Tony had said nothing about a fertility dance). For twenty minutes the drum beat slowly rose to a frantic pace and the bump and grind on stage never faltered. The atmosphere was dense with oozing hormones and had I not had a different agenda I'd have enrolled the next day. The Valley High cheerleading squad came out a poor tenth in comparison. I couldn't help but wonder how the chaperones for the visiting students fared that night.

Dave and I both wanted to explore the highlands but there was no safe place to leave the boat in Lae where the highlands highway began. On a hunch I checked with a freighter docked at Alotau. It was on its way north and the skipper offered us a lift. We secured TR with an extra line to the palm tree and hopped aboard the China Doll. For three days we ate Chinese food and caught up on recent video releases.

I had the address of a contact in Lae. He was a contractor living in a gated and guarded community on the edge of town, which I found to be the norm for white folks here. He gladly put us up for the night but a bout of malaria (also a norm) had pretty well incapacitated him. Even in my book he looked bad. I hope it was all worth it to him. I'd been dosing myself with chloroquinine as a precaution for several weeks. This wouldn't prevent malaria but would lessen the effects if I became infected. We tiptoed from the house the following morning and stuck out our thumbs.

A group of college age kids from Lae picked us up and as they were also touring, their stops were our stops. The highway itself was well maintained and similar to a poor secondary road in the U.S., but it ran through some rough country. At a small roadside fruit stand Dave struck up a conversation with a white guy that had a set of golf clubs in his car. Turns out he was a missionary from New Mexico and gave us a ride up to Garoka, the western most "city" on the highlands plateau. Seems the brethren all hung out at the local country club every day except Sunday. Dave was in his element; not only did he swing a mean stick, but he could also debate religious theology all day long.

Due to the mile-high elevation, nights were downright cold. In our frosty search for an inn we met Leon, a rugby player from the national team. He was a single guy with a fairly large apartment and took it upon himself to be his country's host. He took us to a back street "nightclub" where white people had never been seen, but we were treated with the utmost respect and weren't allowed to buy our own beer. I think it was because we were with Leon who was a local hero. A band played their own brand of what I would term "gutteral disco" and with a little prompting from the chief, the women kept Dave and I on the dance floor till the wee hours.

Leon gave us tickets to a local championship rugby match. I went and Dave played golf. Leon had practice so I was on my own and the stands were full to overflowing with people dressed in everything from suits to revealing tribal paint jobs. Some even carried spears and stone axes. I was one of three white faces in the crowd. There seemed to be a controversy toward the end of the match and when the final whistle blew, the stands emptied onto the field where a major riot ensued. Bricks, arrows, spears and stones flew every which way. Police cars, sirens blaring, rolled into the crowd and the cops let fly with teargas grenades. A guy standing next to me caught a brick along side the head, then out of nowhere a brute in a bulging T-shirt grabbed my arm and yelled, "Follow me." Not one to argue, I ran behind him through the crowd to a gap in the fence, but not before we were both well gassed. Eyes streaming, we ran for about a hundred yards into the bush until we came to a trail. He pointed and said, "The highway," then turned and ran back.

When I showed up back at the apartment, eyes still smarting, Leon almost cried with relief. Apparently several people had been killed in the riot plus many injured and he'd been worried sick. On the up side, Dave hit a par on the front nine and won us a helicopter ride into a remote mining site. It was a spectacular two-hour ride over otherwise impenetrable terrain, and I chose to believe our pilot was an excellent flier as opposed to crazy.

Leon drove an old Pinto that was missing the windshield. We tried to find him a replacement, but there were none available so we filled his tank to say thanks. Repair parts were mostly used stuff from wrecking yards and as we hitched across the highlands, I performed quite a few emergency auto repairs just to keep things moving. Mostly it was carburetor trouble but on one large truck I wired a tie-rod end back together and prayed it would hold till we wound our way down from a steep mountain pass. For all I know it's still going strong.

The end of the line for us was the Baier River bird sanctuary. I'd never seen such incredible plumage. From birds of paradise to cockatoos and hornbills, all were on display, some in cages but many in the wild if you could spot them in the dense foliage. Our return bus ride to Garoka was held up for two days because of inter-tribal warfare on the route. A three-year land dispute had erupted in violent action between two tribes with hundreds of warriors on either side of the road. All dressed in battle finery they used clubs, spears, bows and rocks to beat each other into submission. The only thing out of place was the occasional digital watch. When the bus did make a run for it, we were pelted with rocks from both sides and suffered a few broken windows. I'm sure those windows haven't been replaced to this day.

The health of the economy in New Guinea is apparently measured by the state of the beetlenut market and each town has its own beetlenut market separate from the general produce market. Beetlenut is the local intoxicant much like cava root was in Melanesia. It is mixed with white powdered lime and chewed. I can't deny it gets you high, but it's incredibly bitter and the lime burns the soft tissue inside the mouth - definitely an acquired habit. It also turns your saliva deep red and all the sidewalks in town are stained that color. I was glad to be wearing shoes. Beetlenut and tobacco are both consumed by young and old, starting at 2 years, and the Sydney Herald is the most sought after newspaper for rolling your own. Each page sells for 15 cents in the market.

While waiting for our freighter, I took a side trip to Madan, 200-miles up the coast from Lae. The red dirt road had been pushed through heavy jungle and if it had rained, I believe I'd still be there. There was only one small hotel in Madan and it was full. I found myself wandering through town and came across the fire station. Via pantomime I explained that I too was a fireman from America. They were anxious to know how much firemen were paid in America. That took some time to figure out, but relative to their cost of living, American salaries at the time were comparable. They invited me to sleep at the station with them and I hoped we'd get an alarm, but it was a quiet night.

On my return trip to Lae, I came across a newly cleared field on the side of the road where several villages were having a sing-sing, which is their version of a music festival. With over 800 different languages in New Guinea communication can be a problem, but the one thing they all have in common is the sing-sing. Hundred of natives decked out in costume had gathered for the event. I watched dancing and listened to singing for three hours before the mosquitoes forced me on my way.

Our freighter connection fell through, so we splurged and bought airfare back to Alotau. As I strapped myself in just aft of the cockpit, I heard one pilot ask the other, "What are these switches for?" The other answered, "I'm not sure, but it doesn't matter. We don't use them anyway." Alotau was the last of eight stops, all on remote turf strips so I only had to survive eight landings and we'd be home free. Actually, I was glued to the window the entire five hours absorbing the scenery and thinking what a culture shock these people had gone through since 1930 when the first white men appeared in the highlands.

TR was just as we left her except for a healthy crop of mildew and the dinghy having sunk from excessive rain – remember, this was the dry season. We took on a few stores and sailed north with hopes of reaching the Trobriand Island, home of the dancing high schoolers, and famous for their woodcarvers (sort of like buying Playboy for the articles). Mother Nature had different ideas when half way there non-stop rain turned us back. We did however discover the most remote village of the entire ten-year voyage. My barometer for this was the Animals version of the song "House of the Rising Sun." Wherever I went I used my guitar to make friends and would inevitably play that song whose popularity had reached radio stations far and wide. I could easily spot recognition in the eyes of the listeners. At a small village on the north end of Sanaroa Island, as we sat around a communal fire, I played that song and for the first and only time there wasn't the slightest flicker of recognition on the fifty or so faces gathered there. It seemed fitting that we would now return to civilization.

We found civilization at our next stop near Normandy Island. A group of local evangelists were putting on a series of short plays in an open-air theatre hacked from the bush. It was a hammer-on-the-head presentation of choosing heaven or hell, quite effective propaganda and a serious putdown of all local cultural beliefs. Dave, having spent hours in conversation with the missionaries of all sects at the country club in Garoka, had learned that the true conversion rate was only about 2%. Apparently most of the congregation just likes to get together and sing and take advantage of all the free food and clothing sent by the supporting churches.

TR set new records during the screaming three-day passage to Cairns, Australia. With 20-knot winds on the beam she ticked off 150 miles per day under shortened sail. Although boisterous at times, it never rained. Cairns, the Ft. Lauderdale of Australia, holds the record for the most insane bureaucracy when entering a country. 17 different yet redundant forms dating back to 1901, with questions like, "Are you an English vessel or foreign?" Oh, please!

Fortunately we'd landed a good-sized mackerel on the way in and a couple of thick filets went a long way to expediting matters. To be fair, the poor agent in charge was suitably embarrassed by his country's heedless consumption of forest products and helped fill out the maze of paperwork.

Although we'd arrived in Australia, Sydney was still 1500 miles south against prevailing conditions. But northers blew through at this time of year, and knowing TR's sad performance to weather, we'd drop everything and run whenever there was a hint of a wind shift. Just where we'd hole up was entirely of luck's choosing. Behind one barrier island we got stuck for several days along with half a dozen Aussie yachts. At night they all had an eerie blue light emanating from their portholes. I assumed it was some weird fluorescent light or a no-bug light, but I soon discovered the source was from TVs. The whole idea of TV on boats seemed so foreign to me all I could do was laugh. During a barbie (Aussie for BBQ) on the beach we all made a plan to go hunting wild goats the next day. When I rowed in the following morning all the Aussies were already to go but they all looked surprised when I showed up empty handed. "Where are your guns?" they asked. None of them had a firearm on board but they'd all assumed being a Yank I'd have a full arsenal. It was a lucky day for the goats. I've never carried a gun aboard because, by my own rule, I don't qualify – if you can shoot first, carry a gun – I can't. The gun issue is a popular debate among yachtsmen. I've met all kinds from gunless folks like me to those who wouldn't leave harbor without automatic weapons and hand grenades. My own feeling is that if you have a gun in your hand, the opposition considers you a threat and they don't know your resolve. Most countries require you to turn over any weapons while visiting anyway so they just become liabilities. On another level, guns just seem to invite negative stuff floating around the universe into your life.

Cruising south along the Great Barrier Reef was anything but laid-back sailing. Navigational hazards abound and a sharp eye on the compass is a must. Each night we'd be exhausted from the day's trials. As we sailed from New Guinea, Dave had decided to quit smoking and gave the last of his cigarettes to a delighted lad in a dugout canoe. He hung in there, abstemious, for two weeks but hit a serious wall one evening after a long day's haul. I anchored at the mouth of a river so we could get an early start the next day. At dusk, on the verge of a nervous breakdown, Dave spotted the lights of a boat anchored what I guessed was two miles up the river. Desperate, he launched the dinghy and rowed madly into the dark against a 2-knot ebb tide. At midnight, he dragged himself aboard after a two-hour row against a 2-knot flood tide – all for one cigarette. I vowed to never again take on crew who smoked.

A day later, while Dave was off bumming more cigarettes, I set a pot of beans to cook in the pressure cooker. I'd had this particular cooker for many years but soon after Panama the safety relief valve rusted out and I'd replaced it with a stainless bolt. The main pressure valve was spring-loaded and I always kept a sharp ear to the level of hissing once the pot reached cooking temperatures. An hour into this batch of beans the hissing stopped and I went into the galley to check on the valve. I tapped it and it hissed again. I decided to give it five more minutes and returned to the settee where I'd been stretched out reading. Before I even picked up the book, BLAM! A sheet of searing steam and beans shot from the galley door and sprayed the main cabin everywhere except where I lay. Thirty seconds earlier I'd been standing directly over the pot. The explosion caved in the top of the stove and broke both cast iron burners. Beans blasted through the overhead vent covering the entire starboard deck all the way to the stern. The galley was a nightmare. Every groove in the galley's 2" tongue and groove paneling was pressure packed with slimy beans. The thought of that bean paste hardening in all those grooves drove me like a demon until, using a toothbrush, I'd scrubbed out all the nooks and crannies. Six hours later I made myself a peanut butter sandwich. I now use a cooker with a weighted valve.

From Coffs Harbor (more than half way) south we caught a ride in the Australian current, which ran at a good five knots. Combined with TR's six knots we were making good 11 knots over the ground. The coastal lighthouses almost flashed by. We picked up the glow of Sydney two days out and sailed past the opera house on November 20th. Rushcutters Bay offered a free unlimited anchorage and once the anchor was snug in the mud, I hit the American Express office for a waiting pile of mail.

Among the stack of hey-how-ya-doins, were the divorce papers from Linda needing my signature. I'd kicked that situation around quite a bit over the past 18 months and I felt a certain relief in bringing that chapter of my life to a close. There was also a letter from the San Francisco Linda. Her yacht delivery had fallen through and she wanted to meet me in Sydney and continue the voyage. I'll admit I'd missed her companionship, but there seemed something permanent feeling about her letter that caused me to mull things over for a couple of days before sending her the okay.

Not long after my arrival, Dark Star dropped anchor nearby. They had recently come from New Zealand with "Sonny" a new baby boy as precious cargo. A youngster is a handful and Jeff and Janelle would soon trade the cruising life for a solid land base back in the States, shipping Dark Star back as deck cargo to the Pacific Northwest where she ultimately came under new ownership.

Dave, who had become interested in owning his own boat, found a crew position on a harbor cruise boat that offered him room and board, allowing him to scour Sydney and environs for that dream vessel. Good luck Dave.

Village beauties in Sanaroa

Selling Birds of Paradise for their feathers
in New Guinea

The Land Downunder

"Dig deeper, use a bigger tool!"

The U.S. and Australia are of a similar size and it didn't take me long to figure out that the only way I'd get around efficiently would be with my own set of wheels. It was a green and roomy land yacht, a 1972 Ford Falcon for $800 that would soon be christened the emu-mobile for obvious reasons. Just picking up Linda and all her luggage at the airport made the investment worthwhile.

In San Francisco Linda had taken to decorating yacht interiors for a living, which went a long way to explaining the dubious mass of luggage. She'd been well aware of TR's appointments and they were obviously not up to her new standards. I had no misgivings about losing the Corelle Ware dishes, which in truth don't break, they explode, but I held a certain fondness for the flatware. This was odd collection of utensils each with their own provenance, like the spoon Claude had borrowed from Tom Neale's shack on Suvarov. I finally spoke up when my favorite spatula, which had been with me since I learned to cook, was callously tossed in the trash heap. I knew she'd be able to set a pretty table, not that we did that much entertaining, but it seemed as though the entire character of the boat suddenly morphed into a vacuous trend with no soul. This of course was my token resistance to change that I'd reconcile within the week. Besides, it probably wouldn't be my cooking on display.

My sister Carla, her husband Ross and an old friend, Chris Spanovich, flew from New Mexico for the holidays. We loaded up the Falcon and hit the road for points west, the first being the opal mines at White Cliffs. In 100-degree heat and no AC we drove through miles of dust into a desolate landscape where nothing moved, not even the dust. There were only a couple of weathered buildings, the bar and store, in White Cliffs. I'm sure cold beer was invented for our particular condition. Although it looked like a ghost town, White Cliffs was a thriving underground community hiding from the incessant heat, and like so many ants tunneling away in search of iridescent stone. After a couple of icy Fosters, we entered a cavern where an opalized dinosaur lay on display. The natural history museum in Sydney had offered the guy $10,000 for the creature but the opal value alone was worth far more than that, so here it was attracting tourists for a buck a hit. The dinosaur man took us into his opal mine at the bottom of a thirty-foot shaft that accessed a network of tunnels lit by a few bare bulbs dangling from thin strands of wire. The temperature was a blessed 72 degrees. Armed with worn screwdrivers, we picked away at the gravely surface and lo and behold here were small pockets of opal. Not unlike a reenactment of the scene at Sutter's Mill in 1849, we left White Cliffs with dollar signs in our eyes and plans to stake our own claim as soon as we got back to Sydney. But after a few miles of desolation we asked ourselves, who would want to live in White Cliffs?

At one barren crossroads where we made another cold Fosters stop at a dilapidated lone pub, we were refused service by the black bartender. "Next door, Mate," he said with a tilt of his head. I hadn't noticed another building, but soon found the one building was divided in half, and we had missed the white side. Until that moment, I hadn't realized Australia had a color bar. Carla was put out, said it reminded her of South Africa when she'd been there in the early seventies. There was talk of boycott. America, I pointed out, isn't any different especially in the rural south and all three are derived from the British, so we shouldn't let our own lofty morals prevent us from ordering a cold beer.

The stench of rotting flesh permeated the air along the endless highway as the countless carcasses of kangaroos and emus flashed by, all aflutter with carrion birds. So why did it come as a surprise when a 70-pound emu made a suicide dash in front of our speeding car? A heavy thud and burst of feathers followed by a screech of locked tires brought the Falcon to a hard stop. Siding with the emu, the tow truck driver made a couple of anti tourist remarks as we were hauled to the nearest town for repairs. A new water pump and radiator and a length of rope to hold down the hood and we were good to go. A unanimous show of hands opted for the Barossa valley, aka the wine country surrounding Adelaide. We "tasted" wine all one afternoon driving with increasing deviation from vineyard to vineyard stashing the odd favorite bottle into the boot of the emu-mobile. By days end there were no favorites - they were all terrific.

Accommodation varied along the route, while Linda, Chris and I favored camping, mainly for budget reasons. Ross and Carla, those with real jobs, usually found a local hotel or B&B. We rotated seating and driving, but the center of the back seat was especially brutal. Linda dropped in the popularity polls when she claimed a need to sit up front (the prime seat) due to severe back pain. None of us were all that comfortable, so she didn't get much of a sympathy vote. Pain relievers didn't seem to help Linda's back but Fosters made life for the rest of us more tolerable.

The penguin parade, an odd nightly occurrence at Philip Island drew a pretty good crowd. We stood along the beach at sunset when hundreds of formally dressed birds surfed ashore and waddled through a hundred informally dressed, camera-crazy tourists. I understand now that the tourists are kept well away from the parade grounds.

Carla's zeal for horses was the only thing powerful enough to get us to drive (on the left side, mind you) into downtown Melbourne. Stuffed and encased in glass for all time was the famous racehorse Phar Lap. Not exactly high on my personal list of priorities, but there was a great Chinese food restaurant next to where the formerly speedy equine was on display.

The emu-mobile developed an ominous backfire as we wound our way up and over the Snowy Mountains back to Sydney. The loud pops were limited to the steep uphill climbs so I had every confidence we'd make it back to the boat without a breakdown. Maybe it was this extra bit of stress that put Chris over the top enough to have her knee-length hair dyed purple at a local fundraiser where we'd stopped to check out the festivities. Piercing wasn't a common practice yet.

We spent the early summer Christmas in Sydney Harbor, lounging in the warm sun on TR's deck. The only hint of a southwestern flavor were the two pitchers of margaritas we passed around. Within days our visitors would be back to ice and snow so it was important that they absorb as much heat as possible to see them through the winter.

TR had grown impatient during our absence and now demanded a complete rebuild of her exhaust system and a valve job for the 35-hp BMC diesel. Being a British engine, parts were readily available in Sydney and I was able to pick up a few spares that weren't available in the U.S. I also dressed up TR's mast and boom with four new coats of varnish. And just before we set out for a road trip to Tasmania, we repainted her decks. With the car already packed, the last brushstrokes went on at the boarding ladder so there would be no opportunity to step on the fresh paint, which if we'd stayed aboard would have been inevitable.

In Melbourne, we were confronted with a $450 round trip ferry ride to Tassy so we opted for leaving the car on the mainland and hitchhiking round the island. Like New Zealand, rides were easy even with the two of us, until we arrived near Queenstown, the site of a controversy over a dam that would have flooded the beautiful Franklin River Valley full of old growth timber and stunning landscapes. The locals were for the project as it meant employment, but they lost out to the "greenies" and anyone who looked the least bit radical was looked upon with suspicion. As we walked through town, "Dueling Banjos" played in our minds, as our reassuring smiles grew thin. It was a relief to reach the town limits. We hiked for two hours with no ride in sight and darkness soon to fall. We passed an abandoned lumber mill and were contemplating camping there for the night when a grizzled old coot appeared at the door of a dilapidated shack and beckoned us over. As we neared, the body odor and stale beer about made me gag. "Where'd you two come from?"

"America," we said.

He looked down the empty road, "You been walkin' all the way?" Another face loomed behind the old man, this one much younger. I was thinking we'd best be on our way.

The young one said, "Where you plannin' to sleep? Gets cold

at night."

"Down the road," I said.

The old guy nodded at a beat up camping trailer parked behind the house. "Two good bunks in the sheep wagon."

The young one said, "We were just fixing supper, are you hungry?"

Linda nodded and shrugged off her pack. "Let me help," and followed the men inside. I rolled my eyes and followed her. From the litter of beer cans, it was instantly clear these guys, father and son, had been on a serious binge. I asked, "When was the last time you had a good meal?"

The old man grinned, "Been about a week now."

That set Linda into motion and before they knew it, she had a huge kettle of some kind of mystery stew burbling away on the stove. How she managed with only a freezer full of white bread and four cases of beer, I'll never know. After dinner, we cleaned their kitchen while the son got dad settled into bed. They were the "caretakers" for the old sawmill but had been on the dole for over two years. They had both given up on dreams.

In the morning, the son, grateful but looking haggard, saw us off with a souvenir Queensland tea towel and a partial box of cookies, "to get us through the day."

A white-knuckle ride later that morning got us all the way to Hobart, where friends of friends welcomed us. We walked to the harbor to see if we knew any of the boats in the marina, but none of my acquaintances had made it that far south. Then we entered the yacht club bar. The place was noisy, warm and crowded. I yelled an order for two beers and the place became strangely quiet. I looked around and the guy standing next to me nodded at Linda and said, "She's not allowed in here. She can drink in the members dining room".

I watched the look on Linda's face turn from inquisitive to outrage. "You have got to be kidding. In this day and age?"

An older man at her elbow just nodded. "Sorry, men only, miss."

She turned in a huff and stormed out the door.

I shrugged and said, "She's a bit touchy about chauvinistic rituals," and followed her outside. A roar of laughter came from inside. We found a nice pub down the street with live music. I wondered how they would handle boat crews from the Sydney to Hobart race, which would involve both genders. I saw good potential for a riot there.

Hobart was just waking up to the potential of renovating the old waterfront factories that had lain dormant for decades. Loft condos and artsy shops were popping up around the harbor.

Tasmanian devils do exist, but their nocturnal nature only allowed for daylight sighting in captivity or as road-kill. And no, they don't whirl, but yes, they have ferocious teeth.

We toured the grim remains of the original prison where all the petty thieves and debtors from England were first confined. After the trip from England their stores must have been pretty well depleted and foraging for food must have been tough – not a challenge I would relish. One of our last rides was on an old school bus under the command of an ancient hippie couple. Their rumbling Tassy accent mixed with a raucous engine reduced comprehension by 50%. We did however understand the reason for their current jaunt. They had just poisoned 400 rabbits on their two-acre farm and piled the carcasses onto a huge bonfire and now were driving around to avoid the smell. Ahaa, all those early prisoners must have lived off rabbit.

We found the emu-mobile where we'd left it, somewhat dusty and adorned with a fluttering parking ticket. Seems three days is all you get, but there were no signs explaining this. I filed it in the glove box with a couple of other parking violations that seemed to accrue in the cities.

We drove north beyond Sydney to Coffs Harbor, home of sailing friends, Peter and Jan. By the time we arrived, the emu-mobile had an extreme case of gas, farting at every acceleration. With Peter's help, we rebuilt the top end of the engine, replacing four badly burnt valves. Coincidentally, Peter had an old Falcon parked in his back yard, ready for the wreckers, so I swapped out our crumpled hood for his near perfect one. The white color gave the green car a rogue taxi look.

Jan was a local fitness guru, heading a network of aerobic instructors and hosting a daily TV show. She roped me into teaching a 3-day CPR class for all her instructors. They were all so fit the teaching dummies only lasted one day before the inner springs gave out, and this without the adrenaline of a real emergency. But hey, the way I see it, too much is better than too little.

The day before we were to head back to Sydney, a guy tried to pass us in a residential area just as we turned left. Thankfully no one was hurt but the driver side door really got mashed. The guy handed us a hundred dollars for a replacement door from the wreckers and drove off. I gave the money to Peter and took the door from his white Falcon. Now the emu-mobile looked like a real badass taxi.

Back in Sydney word had gotten out that I was handy on boats. The day we moved back aboard a couple rowed over and asked if I'd do some work on their charter yacht. It sounded like a couple of weeks would see the job done and as we were in no great hurry to leave, I agreed to take on the work. The upshot of the situation was a trade for two self-tailing winches, a little cash and a large sun awning that with minor alteration fit TR like a custom job.

On a hot still day, armed with decent paint brushes and 2 quarts of moss green enamel, Linda and I repainted the emu-mobile prior to reselling the poor beast. Other than a small sag on one door, it came out looking pretty good. The day I placed an ad in the paper however, an ominous thunk came from the transmission whenever it was shifted into drive. How is it some people always come out ahead selling used cars? I sent Linda with the emu-mobile to swim with the sharks on Sydney's automobile row. Unbelievably, she returned unscathed with $350 in hard cash. Seems the first dealer she took it to test drove it but always shifted into low instead of drive and never heard the thunk. She took his check to the nearest bank and never looked back.

I made a last stop at Amex for mail. The woman in charge of mail handed me a thick packet from the Sydney police accompanied by a little smirk. Inside were copies of the six parking tickets the emu-mobile had collected over the last four months with a short note asking me to please come in and see Sergeant so-and-so. Right. I asked the woman to please forward any late mail to the Cairns Amex.

Cyclone season had wound down so we sailed north. Ten miles

shy of Coffs Harbor a wind shift had me out on the bowsprit changing headsails when a rogue wave plucked me off. I was in full foul weather gear with a chokehold on the sail I'd been replacing. Fortunately I hadn't unclipped the last two hanks and I came up hard against TR's hull near the stern. The mainsail drove the boat at three knots and I couldn't risk releasing my grip on the sail. Furthermore, my foul weather gear had filled with water and made impossible for me to climb aboard unassisted. A spare halyard and one of the mast winches driven by Linda's adrenaline-spiked arm hoisted my sodden countenance aboard. They don't call those long bowsprits "widowmakers" for nothing. I started using a harness with a short tether after that. Later, in South Africa, I would make a rigging change that would eliminate my need to go out on the bowsprit.

We made a six-day stop up the river at Bundaberg, where I rebuilt TR's cockpit and installed the new winches. She now had a cockpit combing that tilted out instead of in (I think that had something to do with stiff British posture) so we could actually lounge in the cockpit. The new winches tamed her largest headsails and gave our arms a needed break.

Lady Musgrave is a true coral atoll that marks the south end of the Great Barrier Reef. We arrived with good afternoon light to negotiate the narrow entrance into the lagoon where low tide made it seem like a bathtub. At sunset the wind picked up from the south and by dark blew a full gale. As the 8-foot tide rose a heavy swell crept over the reef. At midnight it was like being anchored in the middle of the ocean. I'd long ago let TR's chain run to the bitter end and hand set the anchor, but it didn't help us sleep. We bailed from the atoll at sunrise and flew north under double reefed sails. 80 miles further on we tucked into the lee of Middle Percy, a barrier island 60 miles offshore. We rolled our guts out until high tide, then, along with a catamaran, slipped into a small harbor that was dry at low tide. We bolted on TR's beaching legs for that event and caught up on much needed sleep. When we awoke, two emus paced around the boat looking for handouts. We hand-fed them bits of dried fruit and they followed us around like loyal pets. A single bloke named Andy who'd gone totally troppo, a common Australian disease in these latitudes, leased the island. Andy was clueless about mechanical things so another yachtie and I repaired the diesel engine that drove his water pump in exchange for fresh fruit and veggies that he grew in abundance. I also traded him a bolt of blue cotton fabric for two tanned wallaby hides that now decorate TR's cabin sole in harbor.

One evening, while dining on the cat, the skipper complained about his Bruce anchor not being reliable. I pointed out TR's 65-pound CRQ plow and said those fateful words, "I never drag anchor." A week later, after a series of rolly anchorages we found a flat harbor in the hook end of a long fishhook-shaped island at the south end of the Whitsunday group, Australia's answer to the Virgin Islands. Tides run ten feet here so we ran out ample scope before setting the plow into the hard sand bottom. At midnight, we were awakened by the crash of dishes tumbling onto the galley floor. I cursed the SOB that must have put out a heavy wake in passing and climbed on deck to give him a piece of my mind. At first I thought I was dreaming, but no, those were real ocean waves breaking over our bow. Land was nowhere in sight and the anchor chain hung vertical. It goes without saying the wind still piped in at 25 to 35 knots, the norm for this time of year. I finally spotted a flashing white channel marker in the far distance, matched the flash pattern to one on the chart, then ran a position line from the compass heading. I was horrified to learn we'd drifted over five miles through a narrow channel spiked with rocky spurs and out to sea. I figure I used up most of my good anchoring karma on that one.

Navigating the Great Barrier Reef required my constant attention to charted details. Linda, perched on the bow, kept a sharp eye for uncharted hazards in the shallow zones. Consumed as I was by external threats, I was stunned to find an even greater danger lurking aboard. Tucked in the pages of one of the cruising guides I occasionally used for reference was a photocopied article about vasectomy reversals. My confusion only lasted a few seconds. Seems I was quite a few moves behind in the chess game of life. I'd been content with taking things a day at a time, but not so Linda who had us married with kids long before she flew into Sydney. When I confronted her with the article she gave me one of those fake remorse looks from behind a fall of dark hair. "They say it's painless."

We were so far out of touch all I could do was laugh. It didn't take me long to explain the reality of the situation from my point of view and I actually thought she understood. What I didn't understand was her stubbornness.

We put into Cairns, my original port of entry, for needed supplies and dental work. I'd had a chronic sinus infection for several weeks and I now felt a tenderness above one of my front teeth where long ago I'd suffered through a root canal. X-rays showed the metal spike used in the original root canal had penetrated into the gum and was now being rejected by my body after 15 years. The dentist reopened the hole in the tooth and tried unsuccessfully to remove the silver spike. I came back the next day for further excavation but after an hour he ran out of time and again sent me on my way, saying if he couldn't get it tomorrow I'd have to have surgery, which meant drilling through the mandible to get at the spike. I was thinking more in the line of having the tooth pulled and a bridge made. Forty minutes into the next day's probe the dentist threw down the little corkscrew looking tool he'd been using and cussed. I panicked. "Dig deeper," I said. "Use a bigger tool. Try at least one more time."

The dentist sighed and picked up a bigger corkscrew. "I don't think this will even fit." But it did and he dug deeper (thankfully the nerve was long dead). A sharp tug and bingo! He got the bastard. A round of antibiotics and a bill for $90 and I was ready to blow town.

I stopped by the Amex office for mail and found another packet from the Sydney police. This time they had dropped the please from their come-in-and-see-us request.

Winds were still consistent at 25 – 35 knots and we flew up the coast day-hopping all the way. At Flinders Island, we met up with a couple of other American yachts also heading north. One of them was Courier, with my old friends Sarah and Parker aboard whom I hadn't seen since the U.S. Virgin Islands three years ago – great party. Parker's stories all revolved around actual sailing and I had to keep reminding myself that some people actually liked it. The intense coastal cruising we'd been doing made me miss the tranquil quality of open water passages where no matter your course there was nothing to run into. There is nothing worse for a boat or my peace of mind than hard ground.

Diving was near impossible in the fortified winds. Visibility dropped to a few feet and quite often we couldn't even row to shore. I began calling it the Great Barrier Grief. I recall one day of lull and being rewarded with a couple of hefty lobster during the ensuing dive, but also noticed an abundance of dead coral due to an infestation of the crown of thorns starfish which kills the coral polyps.

A pamphlet, You and Your Vasectomy, showed up on the bookshelf which led to further disagreement between Linda and myself. She wanted children before age made it impossible, but I couldn't oblige. I was given until Darwin to change my mind.

One month and 17 anchorages later, we rounded Cape York, finally heading west. Eight days later with only one overnight stop because of the inhospitable and poorly charted coastline we entered the approaches to Darwin. Tides run 28 feet and currents over six knots aren't unusual around some of the headlands. At one point while sailing at a full six knots we actually lost ground at the peak of the ebb. That meant TR was moving through the water at over 12 knots and I have never again felt such sensitivity in her helm. The anchorage was deep but with a good mud bottom so even with only a 3-1 scope on the anchor chain at high tide I felt secure.

My first stop ashore was the Darwin Yacht Club where I posted a crew wanted sign. Linda made flight reservations. No way I wanted kids. My second stop was the Amex office where awaited yet another packet from the Sydney police forwarded through Cairns, this time with a demand for my appearance. The girls in the office, a casual and irreverent bunch, got a hoot out of my unshakable plague of tickets. I left them with a few dollars and a forwarding address in the Seychelles for "real mail only."

I had several applicants for the Indian Ocean crossing and after three and a half years on the road I was getting picky about my crew. Ultimately I signed on Diyon, a young, 6'5" Aussie flyer/air traffic controller with a dream to become a mercenary pilot in Africa. We looked into getting a cruising permit for Indonesia, but found the only possibility would be in conjunction with the Darwin

- Ambon race to be held the following month. The long wait and the necessary equipment qualifications dashed those plans.

Diyon was a neophyte sailor and I made sure he understood about the high tidal range whenever he rowed ashore to run errands. The first time out he got it backwards and returned six hours later to find the dinghy hanging high and dry from its 15-foot painter. Luckily he'd locked the oars in place.

The day before departure we hit the duty free shop for beer, booze and a new tape to tape player with which I planned to renew TR's music selection. The beer was hard earned, requiring three different stops around town (Diyon had the use of a friend's car) for the correct rubber stamps on the receipts to satisfy the duty-free part. When at last we had everything stored I asked Diyon how much he paid for the beer, he gave me a funny look and said, "I thought you paid for it." Sometimes too much bureaucracy is a good thing.

Running with a gale

Fritz Damler

Baby at market in Madagasgar

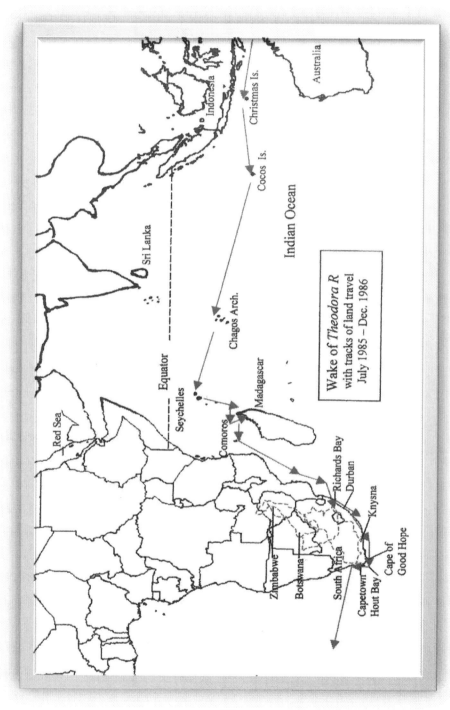

Wake of *Theodora R* with tracks of land travel July 1985 – Dec. 1986

The Indian Ocean

"I think we can ride it out."

The Timor Sea is noted for its high population of poisonous sea snakes whose bite will kill in minutes. We were advised by cruising friends to wear rubber boots in rough seas in case a snake with an attitude washed aboard. Regardless of conditions, Diyon never left the cockpit without a stick in his hand. We had only one rough day and all that appeared on deck was a slimy trio of petit squid. But an attack did come and from an unexpected quarter. One black night as TR ghosted along in a light zephyr I was at the helm when BAM, I was struck in the forehead by something heavy and hard. I yelled an appropriate obscenity and in my dazed condition thought the boom had somehow struck me. Then I heard a thrashing noise at my feet. The perpetrator turned out to be a 12" flying fish. I ate him for breakfast.

Five days out I was below napping while Diyon took the afternoon watch. A firm wind had us moving along at a steady five knots with a moderate roll to port from the quartering sea. There had been no change in TR's motion but something woke me up. I gazed at the deck beams overhead for a while and thought about Ashmore reef, a miniscule glob of coral in the middle of the Timor Sea about 400 miles west of Darwin. I'd plotted our course to pass well north of Ashmore, but my mind played with the idea of the north wind and a south setting current and well, maybe...? Wide-awake, I climbed on deck and walked forward to find Diyon propped against the mast sound asleep. Two miles dead ahead was a frothy white ridge of breakers – Ashmore reef. I nudged Diyon and he jerked awake. I pointed over the bow. When he stood up and saw the line of breakers he did a classic jaw drop and his face drained of color. Need I say more?

One moonlit night as TR churned along wing-on-wing (mainsail to one side, genoa to the other) in a fresh tradewind, I spent part of my watch stretched out on the bowsprit watching an impressive display of brilliant phosphorescence in the bow wave. We sailed into a large school of flying fish that darted out of the waves like silver bullets in the shimmering moonlight. And then as if on cue, a dozen dolphins appeared blazing bright chartreuse pathways around TR's bow. I've never seen a light show to equal it.

A few days later we dropped anchor in Flying Fish Cove on Christmas Island. The last 1000 miles had been a classic downwind cruise and Diyon had barely slept. In a welcome gesture, the small crowd at the boat club shoved a couple of cold Fosters into our hands – no color or gender bars here. The 3500, mostly Malay, inhabitants were supported by the phosphate mine (read bird poop) owned by the Aussie government. Except for the mining part it felt as if we'd landed at a huge adult summer camp with all sorts of entertaining activities like go-kart racing, drinking, movies, golf, drinking, scuba diving, drinking, fishing, dancing and of course everyone loved to knock back a few beers. That first night at the boat club I'd met Marcus, a 25-year-old Australian dental tech built like a fireplug and reputed to be a merciless heartbreaker. The catamaran he'd arrived on the previous year had sunk at anchor in a freak storm and he was looking for a ride out. I signed him on as our third crewmember for the Indian Ocean crossing.

One morning Marcus borrowed a hot pink Land Rover from a friend and we set out on safari to observe a nesting area of the endangered boobie, a rare seabird indigenous to the island. At dusk, not having spotted even the odd feather we were negotiating a seldom-used track in a remote area when the transmission refused to shift into any gear. It was looking like a long walk home in the dark and my erstwhile crew found folly with my attempts to solve the problem with nothing more than a Swiss army knife and a set of rusty pliers. I removed an inspection plate in the floor and not seeing anything obviously amiss, proceeded to bang and jiggle everything within my reach. This had Diyon and Marcus howling until, kachink, the transmission slipped into second gear. The humbled crew agreed to cover my bar tab at the boat club.

On August 10th 1985, we set sail for Cocos Keeling Island, 530 miles west. A thirty-knot tailwind drove us there in three days, a new record for TR. The additional crew made a tremendous difference on the boisterous passage. Watches ran 3 on 6 off but it was clear these boys needed a few basic cooking lessons.

Cocos is an enormous coral atoll and the quarantine station for livestock entering Australia. All imported animals get a six-month holiday in this bit of paradise. Cocos is also a major hub for cruising yachts crossing the Indian Ocean to Africa, Mauritius, Madagascar, the Seychelles, the Red Sea or Sri Lanka. During our week here, 16 yachts came and went. Many were old friends or became old friends, as is the norm in the cruising community. Tales were told and information swapped over an extended period due to the consistent intrusion of the "phantom" rum bottle, which never failed to make an appearance whenever two or more people got together.

Diyon spent his time as the DJ for the local radio station and broadcast all our requests while Marcus and I dove the reefs and played tag with the white tip sharks that roamed the lagoon. When spearfishing, Marcus would go for the fish and I would stand guard with an explosive head on my spear in case the sharks got a little uppity. On one excursion I ran head to head with a 7-foot shark as I swam around a chunky head of brain coral. Startled, I reflexively jerked my trigger finger and blasted an innocent sea urchin. The resulting explosion and shock wave from the 45-caliber bullet scared off everything, including the shark, within a quarter mile. We ate from a can that night.

The BBC radio reports of chaos and unrest in South Africa had me considering the alternative route up the Red Sea to the Med. However, several of the boats passing through Cocos were from South Africa and they assured me I had no worries and that all that radio nonsense had been blown out of proportion. In fact they insisted I come see for myself. The invitation was delivered in such gracious terms, I couldn't say no.

Choosing the central route across the Indian Ocean made our next stop the Chagos Archipelago, a strand of coral atolls 1500 miles west. The southernmost, Diego Garcia, was a U.S. military base and hence off limits except in emergencies. The resulting mild passage lasted two weeks, during which time Diyon discovered his near-white thumb, turning out an array of baked goods from the galley on a daily basis. His favorite (and ours) was cheese muffins, but I didn't realize he'd run through most of our vacuum-packed cheddar (a months supply) in a week.

During the passage I'd read about the clipper trade with China and learned that in this area of the Indian Ocean giant squid, surprised from sleep by a ghosting clipper, would sometimes attack the ship. Some of these squid had arm spans in excess of a hundred feet. I passed this bit of lore on to the crew one evening and that night when I came on deck to spell Diyon, I found him crouched in the cockpit with a machete held firmly in both hands. It took me a couple of seconds to understand why. Then I explained that there probably hadn't been a giant squid spotted anywhere in the world since the advent of the noise polluting steam engine.

Two days from Cocos, after a near calm night that the entire crew slept through with my blessing, we awoke to find TR's topsides and sails enshrouded in what looked like a gray blanket. This proved to be an inch of volcanic ash, and it didn't take long to figure out a belching volcano, hundreds of miles north, in the Indonesian archipelago, was responsible. The three of us spent most of the day sluicing the stuff, a gooey slurry when wet, from all above deck surfaces. It would be months before all trace of the ash disappeared from the multitude of TR's nooks and crannies.

Halfway to the Chagos I caught the largest fish, a 100 lb. yellow fin tuna, that I would ever catch in remote open water. Lacking a freezer, we sliced him up thin, added the appropriate spices and dried the pieces on deck. The jerked meat tasted nearly like beef and provided snacks for two months.

At some point along the way, the subject of hazards at sea came up. I thought stray containerized cargo that had been washed overboard in transit was probably the worst man-made hazard for a small vessel, since they were generally awash and couldn't be seen except by sheer luck on a clear day. Shortly thereafter I noticed that Diyon had taken to sleeping in the forward berth, the shortest and most uncomfortable during a passage. He would scrunch his 6'5" frame into the bunk, brace for the motion and try to sleep.

After three days of this he looked a bit haggard and I asked him why he even tried to sleep up there. He said, "When we hit one of those containers, I want to go out like that," and snapped his fingers. This was from a guy that wanted to fly arms to the rebels in Africa. I assured him that considering our speed (5mph) it wouldn't be like having a head-on with an 18-wheeler but more like hitting a large bump in the road. I pointed out that we might spring a leak and that the chance of even hitting a container was akin to being struck by lightening. The rest of the trip he slept in the aft cabin.

The Solomon Group of islands in the Chagos is a series of six islets strung like emeralds on a coral choker of a lagoon. When the U.S. military took over, in a stellar display of foreign policy, they shipped all the local inhabitants to Mauritius, (a fine how-do-you-do) and now the place is home only to the odd cruising yacht. Two other boats were anchored here and, judging by the growth on their anchor chains, had been here for some time trying to live off the land and almost succeeding. An abandoned (and I'll bet not willingly) copra plantation provided coconut, papaya, lime and breadfruit trees plus a fresh-water well – the previous owners must have been very happy and content. The coral was vibrant and very much alive, making for some awesome scuba dives. Excellent spearfishing kept us in fresh seafood, although the sharks were a bit pushy.

Diyon and his extra rum from Darwin was a big hit with the two other boats, although 20 lbs. of dried fish was not what he had in mind for barter. Ultimately, some cash was produced which led to the exchange of diesel fuel for rice and the rice for flour. In the end everybody won, except the original inhabitants.

After five days in these snug digs, the crew became antsy for a change of scenery (read female tourists) so we pushed on for the Seychelles. In a fresh southeast breeze TR ticked off the 1000 miles in less than 7 days, another passage record. The only mishap was a broken spinnaker pole, the result of my own laziness when an approaching squall didn't appear to have sharp teeth. When Marcus pointed out the dark cloud-line, I gave it a casual glance, surveyed our poled out genoa and the full main and said, "I think we can ride it out." TR damn near became airborne when the wind hit 60 knots.

The volcanic peaks of Mahe hove into sight in the late afternoon of September 9th. I toyed with the idea of heaving-to until morning but my chart, a rough sketch of an old British Admiralty chart, made a night approach look feasible. At 9 p.m. we lined up on the leading lights and eased into the harbor. Out of the night roared a powerful skiff packed with armed soldiers. At first I thought we'd interrupted an attempted coup, but it turned out to be your average welcoming committee of twenty-three. A few years earlier there had indeed been an attempted coup and the guns had been brought in on South African sailing yachts. Anyway, the powers that be were still a bit sensitive about night arrivals by sea. The armed boarding party was a first for Diyon and Marcus and I don't believe they blinked once during the procedure. It didn't help that this AK47 toting security force, average age 16, hadn't taken an NRA gun safety course. I asked them repeatedly to point their guns upward and at one point pinched the end of a fellow's rifle and physically raised the barrel. They politely removed our flare gun and spear guns and anything else deemed a weapon with the promise we'd get them back on departure. Customs and immigration added additional scuffmarks to TR's decks the next morning, then issued us a 6-week visa.

A pile of mail awaited me at American Express. The most notable packet, forwarded from Darwin, was from the Sydney police containing copies of all the parking tickets and a note advising me that the jig was up and there was now a bench warrant out for my detainment should I be stopped in traffic. I wondered briefly if the Seychelles had an extradition treaty with the Aussies − Naaa. But I've since learned that the statute of limitations has expired and I can freely return to the land down under − with a visa of course.

Tourism is the major industry and there was no shortage of beautiful palm-fringed beaches on this terminal green isle. As the crew had predicted, the place was awash with European tourists of female persuasion. One of the local hotels sponsored a "Pirate's Night." We needed no further encouragement. Dressed in Disney fashion we wreaked havoc, took no prisoners and came away with our fair share of giggling wenches. It helped to have a "yacht" in the harbor.

Diyon took a fancy to a woman who worked as an air traffic controller at the local airport and soon shifted berths. Within weeks he would fly to Nairobi and try to peddle his skill as a bush pilot. I learned later that bureaucracy in Kenya had developed to the point that made it impossible for him to follow his dream.

Marcus and I cruised the northern islands, breaking the odd heart and generally debauching our way from resort to resort. At one quiet bay where we'd stopped for R&R, I had just settled into the cockpit with a stiff sundowner when I noticed a strange cloud form over the beach. Within seconds, TR was engulfed in a fresh hatch of swarming black carpenter ants – so much for a quiet night. We slammed the hatches and grabbed the buckets. I thought the volcanic ash was a bitch to get off, but these things were positively tenacious. We stripped every piece of gear off the deck, making sure we didn't leave any stragglers to munch away on TR's hull. Two months later I would find a few we'd missed.

On the island of Praslin, home of the rare coco de mer, a monstrous double coconut weighing in at forty pounds, I witnessed an interesting technical feat. A road crew (two guys with a machete and a shovel) were moving a car-sized boulder from their path. They covered the rock heavily with sticks and underbrush and set it on fire. Thirty minutes later they tossed buckets of seawater on the hot rock. With a loud snap, large fractures ripped through the stone. The two guys carted off the small bits and started another fire. Not once did they break a sweat.

Unexpectedly we were able to secure visas for Madagascar, so we blew off our plans for Mombassa and sailed southeast for Diego Suarez at the north end of Madagascar. One tempestuous night, we blew out a seam in TR's mainsail and limped to Farquar, one of the southernmost islands of the Seychelles. This pristine paradise is now a major destination for fly-fisherman from all over the globe who pay gobs of money to catch feisty bonefish and let them go. But when we arrived, two members of the security force were there to discourage all unauthorized visits, meaning us. I explained our plight and promised we would not trespass beyond a small thatched lean-to where I hoped to repair the mainsail. The senior of the two felt obliged to report our landing to his superiors in Mahe. This ultimately led to a shouting match over the radio between faceless authority and me. I demanded the right of "safe harbor" to make repairs and the jerk on the other end was adamant that I leave immediately. He finally gave us one day, which was all I asked for.

Under the light of a full moon we sailed past the tall, rocky headlands guarding the spacious bay at Diego Suarez. Both navigation lights were out due to a shortage of kerosene.

After the Seychelles where everything required a permit, Madagascar was so laid-back I thought we'd sailed into the Twilight Zone. We even had to go find the port captain to clear in. After signing our names in a giant ledger, we were free to spend the rest of our lives here – finally, a bureaucracy that had come to its senses.

The main thoroughfare in Diego was lined by stately examples of colonial French architecture, now gone to seed as tenement slums since independence in the early sixties. The people seemed at ease with their relative poverty, a fair trade for freedom.

One of the first things I noticed was the lack of trash strewn around. I had carried a plastic bag full of garbage ashore and asked the port captain where I could dispose of it. He nodded toward a shady spot under a nearby tree. It was late morning with a promise of serious heat later on and few people about. I set the bag down under the tree and before I had walked fifty feet, a woman darted into the shade and immediately up-ended the bag. She pawed through the pile extracting glass jars and cans before making a leisurely retreat. Then came the goats. Before we reached the dinghy, the place was spotless. Deprivation – the ultimate in recycling.

Our dollar went a long way especially if exchanged on the black market. A cold liter of Three Horses Beer sold for a buck and a good restaurant meal for five. It had been three times that in the Seychelles but here we noticed a complete absence of tourists, ladies in particular.

I mailed a postcard to a friend in England on the Thursday we sailed from Diego. A Frenchman in line at the post office eyed the post card skeptically and suggested I put it in an envelope. That made no sense to me and I handed it over in its naked state. Later I heard she had received it the next day in the Friday afternoon post – possibly a world record.

Sea conditions were deceptively calm when we sailed out of the bay and we soon found ourselves over-canvassed in a hard beat to clear a reef-strewn lee shore. Green water sluiced down TR's decks. Marcus took a bruising tumble when he tried to lash down some loose gear on deck. We finally managed to tuck a reef in the main and barely cleared the breakers to port. It was definitely my worst departure to date and the snake in my gut danced a jig. As we eased off to a beam reach it was all a piece of cake, even when the wind picked up to forty knots as we rounded the cape. Two hours later, in a dead calm, we motored to our next anchorage, a remote bay on the western shore.

Early the next morning, a procession of villagers skirted the bay and disappeared over a low rise. Shortly, the sounds of revelry came from that direction. Rowing ashore to investigate, we followed a path for a quarter mile and came to a village of thatch and salvaged materials. A hundred or so Madagas were into some serious partying. Live music from an odd reed instrument that sounded like an irate duck and a lively beat from a 55-gallon barrel had everyone stomping their feet. Passed hand to hand was a jug of 100 proof rum that would have burned the valves in TR's engine. They treated us as special guests. On a nearby patch of earth a cow was being butchered, the parts spread in an ever-growing circle on the ground. The dirt and flies were kind of a turn-off. The headman presented us with half the stomach (no doubt a real honor) which we managed to trade down for a section of tenderloin. The celebration, if I understood the sign language correctly, had to do with the cleanup of their local cemetery.

Further down the coast the water turned murky, discouraging us from diving, especially since the locals warned us of big sharks. Our last stop was Hellville, the main town on the off-lying island of Nossi Be. Considered to be a tourist haven, the several resorts only had an average occupancy of 10%. Hellville had to be a marketing nightmare.

The fresh produce market was outstanding, the best I'd seen since Cairns, Australia. At a local restaurant we had the daily special, fruit bat. Yup, tastes like sweet chicken.

On our last day we managed a trip to the mainland to observe the rare Madagascar lemurs, a small furry monkey with a mellow disposition.

Two days later found us 180 miles west, anchored off the town of Zdouzi on the island of Mayotte, a French possession in the Commoro Islands. Several hundred French Foreign Legionaries were stationed here. Marcus and I were the only ones ashore without a butch haircut. We met some of the legionaries and they seemed like nice enough guys, but I couldn't help wondering what sinister crime, if any, they were running from. From what we were told, no matter what crime may have been committed, if you are not apprehended before you join the Legion, you receive a new identity and no civilian court can touch you. A five-year commitment is required upon joining. For further info, check out their web-site at foreignlegion.com.

TR carried two 20lb. bottles of propane, one of which was empty and the other nearly so. I had shared half a tank with a desperate cruiser in the Seychelles, fully expecting to find propane on Mayotte, but to our disappointment there hadn't been a supply ship in for over a month – imagine that.

The rainy season arrived with a vengeance, which meant cyclones were not far behind. The east coast of Africa was pretty much off limits without special visas, so we set sail for Durban, 1200 miles south down the Mozambique channel. We took it as a good omen when a 25 lb. mackerel swallowed the meat-hook as we sailed through the reef. The next ten days were hell. TR suffered a bout of suicidal depression and tried her damnedest to sink. Twenty to forty knot headwinds against a 2-knot current jumbled the seas and plagued us for days. Even with shortened sail the strain on TR's mast step was such that her bilge needed pumping on the hour. This wasn't too bad until the electric pump packed it in and we resorted to the hand pump, which translated to 200 strokes an hour. Four days down the channel we ran out of propane, and meals became rather grim. Ramen noodles re-hydrate well without heat, but don't try it with rice or pasta.

Marcus suffered a remarkable shiner when the sail he was wrestling on deck got away from him. We wore harnesses whenever out of the cockpit, as the seas were totally unpredictable.

Two years later, a good friend of mine would be lost overboard sailing this stretch of water.

Supertankers were not an uncommon sight, appearing ghostlike out of the mist, fully laden with black gold from the Persian Gulf. I called one once on the VHF to make sure TR was showing up on his radar. The captain said, and I kid you not, "Wait a minute, I'll turn it on and see." I'd always wondered how these monster ships, with state of the art electronics, occasionally managed to collide with other ships or run aground.

Two days of favorable winds brought us to within ten miles of Richards Bay, our first stop on the South African coast. But just to let us know who was boss, a front moved in from the southwest and beat us up for an extra 5 hours. At no time since the beginning of this ten-year cruise had I been more relieved to make landfall. It was mid October of 1985 and TR would sit on a mooring at the Zululand Yacht Club for the next five months.

Drying Tuna

Africa

"Drink up Fritz, it's just another bomb."

Idling up to the dock at the Zululand Yacht Club I was overjoyed to find my friends, Sarah and Parker from the yacht Courier, whom I hadn't seen since Darwin. It was one of those moments when the high one feels after an extreme low is spiked to the level of sheer delight. Sarah had a decidedly pregnant bulge and planned to have the baby in S.A.

Within a week there were twenty-five foreign yachts in the harbor with the intention of spending the cyclone season there. Between that and the recently devalued Rand I had strong incentive to stick around. Richards Bay is also an industrial port for the export of coal and wood pulp and seemed like a good place to do the needed repairs and upgrades on TR. After four years and three oceans she was ready for some serious TLC.

Marcus took advantage of the weak Rand and purchased a 30-foot sloop, so I soon had TR to myself again. My biceps were a testament to the work TR needed on her mast step. Marcus and I had each put in over 25,000 strokes on the bilge pump in the Mozambique Channel and I no longer considered TR seaworthy. But before the work began, my mother and her husband Jack flew down for another visit.

We hit the tourist trail, taking in all the game parks in Natal, driving the coastal, "Garden Route" to Capetown and finishing the trip on the "Blue Train" to Johannesburg.

The highlight of our game park excursions came while following a dry riverbed from a dirt track on a high bluff. As we crawled along at idle speed, my foot riding the brake, our attention was drawn to the tracks of a large animal that had recently crossed the riverbed in our direction. I eased the car forward, peering down the slope of the bluff with hopes of spotting whatever it was that made the tracks. A sharp intake of breath from the back seat caused me to look up. Not five feet from the front of our compact rental stood a huge black rhino, head lowered, ears twitching. Up close that horn took on sinister proportions. I fumbled for reverse and almost got stuck in the sand in my panic to vacate the premises – definitely not a petting zoo.

One evening we were invited to a Zulu kraal where after consuming a good dollop of their "beer" made from corn, I was coaxed into participating in a traditional war dance where legs are raised high and slammed to the ground. The third time my right foot hit the hardpan I ripped the cartilage in my knee. I was on crutches for three weeks.

In Capetown I went to a doctor specializing in sports medicine for an opinion about my knee. Professional visits had a state controlled fixed price of $10. He sent me for X-rays. This entailed a dozen pics taken with the usual machine, then the radiologist opened a sterile tray and injected radio opaque dye into the knee. There followed a series of 32 more pics from a rotating machine then back to the first machine for another 6 pics. Unable to contain my near apoplectic concern for the cost of the X-rays I asked the Tech if she had any idea what the bill might be. She said, "I'm not sure, but I know it's expensive." I broke out in a cold sweat, thinking of the measly $200 I had in my pocket and the $15 Casio watch on my wrist. By my American standards, I had already spent over a thousand. I had to wait a half-hour for them to prepare the bill, which upset the office routine. They had wanted to send me the bill even after I explained my transient status (tempting). The final reckoning came to a whopping 92 Rand, which translated to $35. These folks had no idea what expensive means to an American. It also makes a strong argument in favor of foreign travel for medical care. The doc told me if the torn meniscus didn't heal on its own I'd eventually need surgery. But if the tear stitched itself together I'd probably be fine. As of 2005 I haven't booked a surgery flight to Capetown.

Weather patterns at the cape usually move from the southwest to the northeast. Since we drove in the opposite direction along the Garden Route weather changes when they came were fast and didn't last long. This worked in our favor whenever a belt of rain clouds moved through, bringing an intense freshness to the already lush foliage. Tropical plants that I'd always considered indoor plants grew in wild abundance all along the coast. Rarely did we have the air conditioning on so ever-changing fragrances wafted through the open windows. The day we took the tram to the top of Table Mountain, the tablecloth was on, meaning we were enshrouded in a damp fog. Erratic winds buffeted the cloud layer giving us snapshots of Table Bay, Capetown and the cape peninsula.

The Blue Train is touted as the most luxurious train in the world and I have to admit it would be hard to top. The 24-hour smooth, quiet ride winds through desolate land known as the great karoo, where the famous Kimberly diamond mine coughed up all those wedding rings. Three elegant meals were served, a coat and tie affair, and the silver had a blinding sheen. My cabin had its own spa tub so after several glasses of fine wine from the Stellenbosch region around Capetown I took a long soak and had no trouble sleeping. Shortly after a leisurely breakfast the vast mine dumps around Joburg appeared, resembling high mesas of rust and gold.

Connie and Jack flew back to the US from here and I'd had my share of the good life. I returned to the boat for the Xmas holidays and see to TR's demands. I first removed all the interior joinery around the mast, which included the head and galley. I was shocked to find that the previous owner had cut away a good portion of a primary floor timber, one that supported the mast step, to accommodate the shower pan. No wonder the old girl leaked. I found some sheets of ¼" stainless steel at a salvage yard and cut five pieces that bolted into the oak frames for and aft of the mast. On these I bolted a 6-foot section of 2"x 6" channel and made a new collar to accept the mast. With the mast load now spread over a wide area TR never again took on water even in the heaviest seas.

Many of TR's original iron fittings had lost their galvanizing and were in a messy stage of corrosion. The devalued Rand gave me the opportunity to have those fittings remade in stainless steel. When I removed the bracket supporting the bowsprit and lifted the 12-foot timber from its oak pad I found a colony of carpenter ants turning good wood into sawdust. Remember those ants from the Seychelles?

The various projects took over 6 months to complete and I interspersed them with excursions throughout southern Africa. I bought a 1981 Audi for $1200 and lit out for Kruger National Park, South Africa's largest game park. I stopped in Joburg to pick up Veebika, a woman I'd met through friends in Durban. She had never been to Kruger and agreed to accompany me on the five-day excursion. Park rules demand that you stay in your car and not feed the animals. At night we were in a fenced enclosure to keep us safe from the wild beasts. We both had tents and the first night after setting up my little dome tent I asked her if she wanted help setting up her pup-tent. She gave me a, are you kidding? look and said, "We won't need it." By the second day I was convinced I had the wildest beast of the bunch locked in the car with me.

We never came close to running over a rhino, but we saw our share of the big cats including a leopard and cheetah. The most interesting thing we came across was a family who hadn't paid attention to the "don't feed the animals" rule. As a result of handing out snacks to a group of baboons they were now in violation of the "don't leave your car" rule. Apparently the baboons didn't believe these folks had run out of handouts and proceeded to rip the doors off the car in their search for the truth. We took the displaced family aboard and shuttled them to the nearest ranger station, but not until their car and its contents were spread over half the park. The kids were delighted – mom and dad were in tears.

Kruger has its own abattoir to process and can all the meat from culled animals. The brightly-labeled products are sold in park stores. I took advantage of the strong dollar and bought two cases each of canned elephant and Cape buffalo. Generally I am disgusted by most canned meats with all the questionable additives, but these were solid chunks of pure lean meat and used sparingly would last over two years.

The Kruger trip left me with a serious desire to have a more in-your-face safari experience, the macho me-and-my-Swiss Army knife type of thing. On my return to Richards Bay, with some like minded cruising friends, Don and Muriel, I organized an excursion to the Okavango during the dry season later that year. But first, a group of us drove north to Zimbabwe. When I asked my friend

Veebika if she'd like to go, she dropped a fifty-pound hint at having a new beau. Oh well, there's something to be said for a good night's sleep, or at least that's what I chose to believe.

Peggy, an ex-Rhodesian, now living in Richards Bay, acted as our guide. She had spent over fifty years on a farm near the capital now called Harare. The only problem was that she had lived through the Rhodesian war years when the blacks had decided they had had enough of the imperialist white man's rule. Many of her friends in the outlying farms had been murdered and she was understandably a bit nervous when we drove through the more remote areas. At one picnic stop she refused to leave the car and broke down in tears when a car with three black Africans pulled up to ask directions. Don, Muriel and I tried to convince her that the politics had mellowed over the years, but her phobia was too deep for our homespun therapy. We offered to cancel the trip, but she would nave none of it. After that crying episode the only hint we had of her occasional discomfort was an uncommon silence.

Again I was struck by the artistry of local crafts people. The women in particular displayed amazing talent with crocheted bedspreads and tablecloths from the heavy cotton string used in the tobacco industry. Reed baskets were also a favorite, some of which were water tight and nearly indestructible. Muriel and I filled the trunk with our special finds.

The most attractive town we had the pleasure to visit was Bulawayo, with its wide double avenues originally designed to handle a U-turn by a twenty oxen team. Majestic jacaranda trees now lined the walks and central medians. Ivory carvers here had recently received a number of large tusks from an elephant cull carried out at the Whanke game park, and were turning out some really exquisite pieces, like a pride of lions on a kill or miniature herds of gazelle. The culled ivory was the only legal ivory available. Every piece was documented as a deterrent to poaching. However, the park rangers were instructed to shoot poachers on sight, which seemed to me an even more rigorous deterrent. The elephant herd at Whanke, 25,000 strong, is one of the largest in Africa. Being restricted to the park, the numbers had to be kept under control since elephants even in small numbers are amazingly destructive, ripping out entire trees for a few top-leaves. One area, where a recent herd had passed, looked as though a real estate developer had run amok with a few D-9 Cats.

At a distance of 50 miles a plume of white mist left no doubt as to the location of Victoria Falls. Aptly called "The Smoke that Thunders" by the Matabele, it is where the Zambezi River plunges into a deep rift in the earth. Emerging wet and exhilarated from a cliff edge view (no fences or guardrails here) I had renewed my respect for the awesome powers of Mother Nature. The deep thunder reminded me of gigantic surf breaking on a coral reef.

We stayed in a cottage a couple miles upstream of the falls and in the evening we could hear the snort of nearby hippos. Unfortunately, Muriel failed to keep the door firmly closed and a marauding gang of a dozen monkeys invaded our lodging. After two hours of frantic screeches and mindless destruction Don finally managed to drive them out with an aerosol can of wasp killer, but they took most of our food with them. Don and I had side-aches from laughing. Muriel and Peggy were not amused.

The Matopos, a mountain range comprised of massive stylistic boulders, is where Cecil Rhodes is buried. Peggy was horrified to learn the locals had pissed all over his grave, whereas Don and I could understand the African point of view. Rhodes never found any diamond here but there is certainly a powerful energy flow to the place, as if there was an important mystical lesson to learn. Unfortunately we left the area before I discovered what that lesson might be. Someday I'll be back.

In a remote area near the Matopos, an acquaintance of Don's that ran safaris all over Zimbabwe, was putting the finishing touches on a new bush camp with a tree house theme. We were his first unofficial guests and dined that night on grilled warthog. At ten p.m. with no moon the blackness was complete. In the distance a lion coughed. Elephants crashed through he bush less than a hundred yards from the camp. We climbed into an old Land Rover with no top and eased, without lights, towards the noise. Our guide warned us not to speak and rolled right up to an old bull whose silhouette appeared out of the darkness only inches from the Rover's grill. Then he turned on the lights. My heart about stopped. That bull could have plucked me from the front seat with ease. The Rover's headlights ultimately won the staring contest and the elephant wandered off in search of more food.

After the border crossing back to South Africa, Peggy visibly relaxed, but the trip had definitely taken an emotional toll. It would be her last trip to Zimbabwe. But it was also a time of strife in S.A. Nelson Mandela was still a political prisoner. The U.S had instituted economic sanctions against S.A to encourage an end to apartheid − (I sensed a little hypocrisy there). Intertribal violence in the townships seemed a daily occurrence and necklace killings, (a burning car tire placed around the neck of the victim), was the new fashion of anarchists. AIDS wasn't even an issue. From my perspective it was clear that the white government was on its way out and that the country would be going through a tough and violent growth period. For the most part I was personally unaffected by this political upheaval. That changed in Durban.

Back in Richards Bay I reassembled TR's interior and reset the mast and rigging. She also got a fresh coat of paint and with her new fittings could really turn heads. Once the work was done I'd had enough of the boonies so when the seasonal yachts headed out I moved TR down the coast to Durban. The Durban Yacht club is right downtown and would be my home for the next few months.

A couple of days after I'd snugged alongside the visitor's jetty, my friend Harry, a jolly, fast-talking Irishman took me out on the town for a music blitz. Our second stop featured a live rock band visible/audible through the street-side window and the place was jammed. We found space well back at the bar and ordered rum and cokes. Just as I picked up my glass, an explosion ripped through the club. Broken glass raked the crowd. A wall mirror behind the bar shattered. In the eerie silence that followed, Harry turned to me and said, "Drink up, Fritz, it's just another bomb." Being from Belfast, that was easy for him to say. It was my first frontline experience with terrorist violence and I choked down the rum. Then the screams started. The bomb had been in a vehicle parked directly in front of the bar. Several band members and a few patrons were killed and plenty injured from flying glass. Windows from surrounding high rises had also shattered and deadly shards of glass rained down on the street. I slipped into paramedic mode for a couple hours until the worst of the injuries had been carted off to the hospital. Welcome to the big dysfunctional city.

Just after the bomb incident, my sister, Liz, announced her plans to be married. As a surprise present, I flew to Albuquerque, unannounced, for the wedding. Liz had once asked me what I did for a vacation, well this was it. I partied for two weeks until complete exhaustion threatened to hospitalize me. It was great to see old friends and family for a few days, but TR was now my home and I was soon homesick for her quirky moods.

My plane ticket allowed me a stopover in England on my way back. I took the train out to Maldon in Essex to Cook's shipyard where TR had been built. They were still doing some traditional construction but most of their work these days was repair and maintenance. The original boat sheds had burned down during WWII, along with all the construction and line drawings of TR's hull – bummer. I had hoped to obtain copies and build a scale model of TR one day. The one old-timer who had actually worked on TR had taken the day off and I missed the possibility of a few good yarns.

A lady with brilliant red hair, who I had met in the Seychelles, toured me around Devon for a few days. She also confirmed the overnight delivery of the postcard from Madagascar. We stayed in rural farmhouse B&Bs where the massive English breakfast carried us through the entire day. I came away with an addiction to Devonshire clotted cream, which of course went well with my addiction to red wine.

On my return to Durban, I learned that my friends Sarah and Parker were now the proud parents of a baby boy with dual citizenship. Their plan was to sail back to the U.S. with Parker Jr. as the new deckhand. Grandpa and Grandma were not pleased.

I hooked back up with Don and Muriel for the trip to the Okavango. Due to a report of horrific roads, we rented a VW van in Joburg and drove the 600 miles to Maun in northern Botswana, where the Kalahari absorbs the Okavango River delta. The trip took an extra half day because of the numerous military roadblocks. We were never quite clear as to what they were looking for or guarding against.

We flew the final 60 miles to Chiefs Island where a loose-run outfit set us up with two guides and their mocorros (dugout canoes). We packed ten days of food, mostly grits, rice, powdered eggs and sauce mixes, then poled into the far reaches of the delta. Being the dry season, mosquitoes and the tsetse fly were no problem. However, bathing was a bit of a risk with crocodiles and hippos sharing the tub. The water was perfectly clear and drinkable. One of the guides had a hatchet and I had my Swiss Army knife, but other than that all we had for protection was our wits. And at the beginning those were none too sharp. Our guides got a hoot out of our desire to sleep inside a sleeping bag in a tent. They slept under a thin blanket next to the fire, ready and unencumbered to run for the nearest tree if threatened by a hippo, lion or buffalo. I took the hint, plus it made setting up camp a real breeze. Don and Muriel toughed it out in their tent.

Early one morning Don and I tiptoed out of camp and hiked through the tall grass to a knoll about a mile off. The wind was at our face as we crawled to the top of the rise and the air was thick with a barnyard smell. We took a peek. Less than a hundred yards away a herd of over 500 Cape buffalo moved sluggishly along the riverbank. Thankfully we were downwind. We had been warned that Buffalo, when threatened, will charge a suspected enemy en-mass.

Later that day we came across a pride of lions feasting noisily on some unlucky beast. The bush was thick and one of the guides and I tried unsuccessfully to get a photo, but at fifty feet we chickened out. This was definitely my kind of safari. I'll never be able to go to a zoo again.

Our days were spent bushwhacking for miles on the larger islands in the delta or poling through the vast maze of waterways. We shared the space with all manner of wild creature, from the graceful giraffe to herds of elephant and countless varieties of antelope. At night the chuckle of hyenas and the screech of baboon or chatter of monkeys would lull us to sleep. We would awaken to an orchestra of birdcalls and the crackle of a rekindled fire. It was a magical time for all of us and would remain forever a highlight in my own life experience.

A mechanical failure on the plane gave us the opportunity to make the run back to Maun in a speedboat. Slaloming at forty knots through grass choked waterways, dodging the odd hippo was even better than the Disney jungle ride.

On our return to S.A, Don and Muriel took delivery of a new 47-foot sailboat that they planned to finish out themselves over the next year in Richards Bay. We promised to stay in touch. Later, when I reached Gibraltar I would learn that on their maiden voyage to the Comorro Islands Don was lost overboard in a micro storm off the coast of Mozambique. Muriel would lose a battle with cancer a year later.

When the time came for me to sell the Audi, there were no buyers except Len, the manager of the Zululand Yacht Club. In exile from Zimbabwe where he had substantial holdings, he wanted to pay me in Zim dollars. Len's offer was generous but what would I do with Zim dollars outside of Zimbabwe? Then I remembered those ivory carvings I'd seen in Bulawayo. Len gave me a check that he said his bank manager in Harare would cash for me. A friend and I drove north and I used my American Express card as proof of foreign currency when we entered Zimbabwe. In a private office at the bank, I was handed the cash and told to keep the transaction quiet – what transaction? Unfortunately there were no ivory carvings as they'd all been sold and there were no more tusks available. But there was a lot of ivory jewelry in the shops. We drove south with a sack of carved ivory jewelry and a faked Amex receipt as proof of foreign currency used for the purchase. We made it through Zimbabwe customs okay but only had five minutes to cross the bridge to the South African side before the border closed for the night. S.A. had recently placed a heavy duty on ivory coming into the country. I wasn't about to go through all the hassle of placing my purchase in bond and taking delivery in Capetown when I left the country. My friend drove slow as I stuffed all the jewelry into an open space behind the glove box. We had to do some fast talking at immigration because for some reason neither of our reentry visas were in order, but we were able to place the blame on the office in Durban. At customs, there was a car parked out front with the engine running and a harried looking woman in the driver's seat. We entered the office and the officer asked for the papers for the Audi. I returned to the car and when I opened the door to look for the papers, my eyes went straight to a huge pile of ivory jewelry that had dribbled down from inside the dashboard. I looked up and met the eyes of the woman in the nearby car. She gave me a quick smile. I think I smiled back. I found the needed papers and turned off the overhead light hoping the jewelry would disappear. I met my friend and the customs officer coming out the door. The customs man gave the papers a cursory look and said, "My wife is waiting so I don't have time to search your car, but I know you've got some biltong, (jerked wild game) enjoy it." This time I gave his wife a big smile and a wave. When I ultimately returned to the states, ivory jewelry was so politically incorrect as to be almost worthless. Next time I'll just give the damn car away.

Just before I sailed from Durban, a friend of my sister's, Kim, joined TR to crew around the Cape of Good Hope to Capetown. The seas around the cape can be treacherous when a southwest gale blows against the swift Aghulas current, so I set aside plenty of time to pick our passages. The first 3-day leg to Port Elizabeth made an old salt of Kim. A northerly gale pushed us on our way followed by dead calm. TR's injection pump broke a shaft and left us bobbing around in the shipping lanes with no means of power. That night a freighter bore down on us and wouldn't respond to our radio calls. At a quarter mile, when the black hulk of the ship was visible in the dark I flashed their bridge with a portable spotlight and Kim rapidly flicked the masthead light on and off. At the last minute, the ship turned to port and we rocked in its wake. Soon, a light southerly sprang up and we got within ten miles of port when it turned into a full gale. Under double-reef main and stormsail, TR bashed her way into the lee of the headland and at midnight anchored just outside the harbor breakwater. I was proud to note that she hadn't taken on any water and the bilge pump was silent. The next morning we sailed into the harbor with a light north wind and tied up at the visitor's dock. It took a week to get the parts for TR's injection pump. While we waited, Sarah and Parker and Parker Jr. stopped in on their way to Capetown and beyond. But Murphy played a classic trick. Parker motored to the jetty with the intention of using reverse gear to lay Courier alongside, but when he shifted gears nothing happened. He threw his arms up in total surrender as the vessel plowed into the jetty and TR's stern. The act of throwing one's arms up is about as close as it gets to having brakes on a boat. Most of the damage was to Courier's bow pulpit but a few persuasive hammer strokes made for a "good enough" repair. The family would return safely to the U.S. in April.

Kim and I left for Knysna, 120 miles down the coast, in a light easterly. On arrival it was low tide and impossible to pass through the high headlands guarding the harbor, as the sea broke across the entire entrance. While we waited offshore for the tide to rise a heavy bank of fog moved in and the forecast was for a southerly gale. I was in touch with the local sea rescue group by radio and they reported that the passage through the heads would soon be deep enough and was clear of fog. Getting to the pass was another story. Visibility was less than thirty feet, but I had a compass bearing towards the entrance. Under power, we eased through the fog toward the coast until Kim, standing on the end of the bowsprit, spotted breakers on the rocks dead ahead. I turned parallel to the coast and noticed that my radio signal became quite strong as we motored past the opening between the two headlands. As soon as it faded I reversed course until the signal was once again loud and clear. I turned towards shore and rode the swells blindly into the pass. We burst from the fog into brilliant sunshine centered perfectly between Knysna Heads. That was not a move you would learn in sailing class. An hour later the gale blew as promised but we were safely anchored in the lagoon.

The gale sputtered out after three days and we made a break for Mossel Bay, another overnighter before reaching the cape. At dusk, just after we entered the harbor, gale force winds kicked in from the west. TR was tied to the high concrete commercial wharf and threatened to snap her docklines or rip out her cleats when 4-foot seas rolled into the harbor and she bucked like a tethered stallion. At times her bowsprit rose beyond 45 degrees. How we escaped unscathed I'll never know. That was one long night. Near dawn the wind died completely and I got ready to boogie, but TR's transmission had frozen in reverse. The folks on a South African yacht who had shared the previous night's experience offered to tow us out. I accepted and we were shortly under sail in light easterlies. I soon discovered the transmission gearbox had run dry of oil. Where it went, I hadn't a clue. I dumped in 2 quarts of 90-weight and she was good to go.

When we reached "The Cape of Storms" we were under diesel

power in pond-flat seas. But that soon changed too and we rounded the Cape peninsula, aka "False Cape" in a roaring easterly gale under storm jib alone. On our dawn approach to Hout Bay the high surrounding terrain had created horrendous downdrafts in excess of 100mph, forcing us to stand off a few miles until the winds let up. When we finally made landfall I noticed that the way the breakwater was situated, those severe downdrafts would blow straight into the harbor entrance. And wouldn't you know the only available mooring was on the end of a finger dock that faced said entrance. Fortunately someone had had the foresight to plant a 5-ton concrete mooring block 50ft. beyond the end of the pier so TR was kept a safe distance from the large metal cleats on the jetty. I found out later that the additional mooring block was installed after a friend of mine almost had his steel-hulled yacht sunk by the wildly bucking jetty when those downdrafts blasted into the harbor.

The concrete block was put to the test two weeks after my arrival. At midnight (always) an easterly gale brought the downdrafts roaring into the harbor. There was only one other person in the marina living aboard at the time and the two of us spent the wee hours on our hands and knees crawling around on the madly flailing piers retying chaffed docklines on most of the unattended boats. The block held and TR survived without a scratch. At dawn, there was so much salt caked on all exposed surfaces in and around the harbor it looked as if it had snowed.

I found a T-shirt shop in Capetown and ordered several dozen shirts printed with a custom logo of TR under sail on the front and "1980s WORLD CRUISE" on the back. These I would later hand out to repay the many acts of kindness shown me, plus they also took care of my wardrobe for the next three years.

Hout Bay, ten miles south of Capetown would be my last stop. The Whitbread round-the-world racers had filled up the Capetown Yacht Club, which was fine with me, as Hout Bay was far more quaint and picturesque. Kim continued on her world tour from here. I think she'd had just about enough of the sailing life. I awaited the arrival of my old friend, Chris Spanovich, who was currently exploring West Africa and would join me for the South Atlantic crossing to Rio.

During the last year I'd met a whole slew of South Africans, many of whom lived in the Capetown area. Rarely a day would go by without an invitation to some outing or dinner party. Several times a week TR would carry a boatload of new-found friends on picnic excursions or a sunset cruise. Life was good. But by the time Chris showed up I had itchy feet and I could tell by the way TR tugged at her dock lines she too was ready for another crossing.

Basket weaver – The Okavango

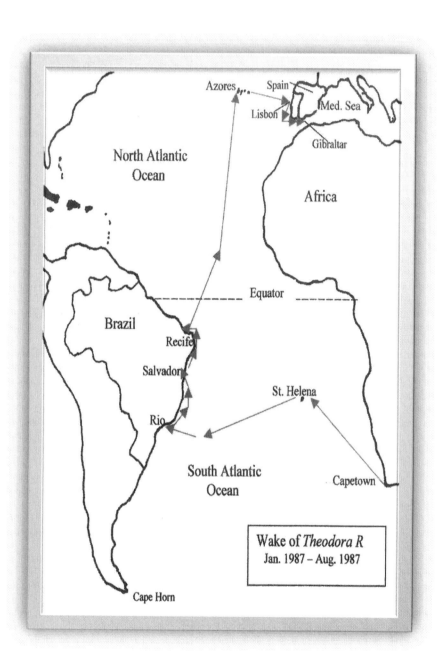

Fritz Damler

Atlantic Wanderings

"All roads lead to Dot's cafe."

TR nosed into the South Atlantic swells in early January of 1987, our sights on Rio with a stop at St. Helena. Chris and I had spent a crazy week provisioning and saying goodbye to now old friends and despite the serpent squirming in my gut it was good to break free of the land-bound sirens. The moderate southerly grew steadily over the next 12 hours until TR frolicked along under reduced sail in a near gale with low scudding clouds and intermittent rain. Curled in the cockpit, Chris's participation was reduced to the occasional moan and Bill earned his keep, steering an accurate course during the three-day blow.

Finally a morning dawned with sunshine and flat seas. The world seemed a cheery place as TR ghosted along at 3 knots. Chris rose from the dead and her appetite returned with a vengeance. The galley, once again a habitable space, churned out food for the soul.

During a lull we fired up the iron genny. An hour later Chris smelled something burning. I jerked open the engine cover and a black cloud of acrid smoke poured out. Flames licked at the wiring around the starter. Having spent many years as a volunteer fireman, I could survey what is considered an alarming situation aboard a small wooden boat with objectivity. Otherwise I might have been in total panic and grabbed the dry chemical extinguisher which makes a god-awful mess. I took a deep breath and blew like it was my fourth birthday and still believed I'd get my wish. It worked and I found where a wire from the solenoid had vibrated loose and caused a short. The solenoid was history. Thankfully I was able to rig things so TR could be started without one because nine months would pass before I found a replacement.

Dirty weather moved in a few days before our projected

139

landfall at St. Helena. Visibility dropped to less than two miles and I only got quick glimpses of the sun. My celestial navigation skills were still a bit rusty after a year of coastal hopping (use it or lose it) and I would have preferred clear, dry air and a few star shots to guide us in. Luckily there were no outlying obstacles and I stressed over nothing because the black rock of the island loomed out of the mist as predicted. The rolly open roadstead anchorage was 80 feet deep over a rocky bottom. I rigged TR's small plow anchor with a length of chain and plenty of nylon rode and she held fine even in gusty winds. For most South Africans, who are accustomed to picking up a mooring, this was often their first experience anchoring – not what I'd call ideal learning conditions. During our stay one couple went ashore for the afternoon and returned to find their boat missing. Locals in a fast runabout raced down current and found the vessel adrift eight miles out.

With no airstrip, St Helena was the ultimate remote outpost whose residents felt lucky if the supply boat came in once a month. No wonder the English interred Napoleon here.

Tarzan would have felt right at home trying to get ashore. The landing was a deep notch cut from a rock wall over which a stout beam was mounted and from this dangled four thick ropes. I would ease the dinghy alongside and on the top of the swell, Chris would grab one of the ropes and swing ashore. I would follow on the next swell, then we'd drag the dink up a short flight of stairs. This landing was a source of constant amusement for the locals who, perched on the high rocks, waited for some poor sailor's timing to be off.

In the absence of anything close to flat, our legs got a serious workout. We hiked to Napoleon's last digs, a cute cottage with a killer view, and I for one thought he did okay for someone who caused the English so much grief. We also met St. Helena's oldest resident, a 200-year-old tortoise the size of TR's dinghy, named, I'll give you a hint, starts with N.

Fishing is the most profitable pastime for the majority of islanders. The English residents have all the cushy government jobs. I'd met Freddy, one of the fishermen, in Capetown and he took us out for a day of hand-lining in 600 feet of water. We came back with rubber arms, three fat tuna and a 100 lb. marlin. Freddy pulled in the anchor. I've never been real big on the sport side of fishing, my enthusiasm being pretty much limited to the potential meal factor.

Where the one road that winds into the far corners of the island plunges to the harbor was a sign that read, "All Roads Lead to Dot's Cafe." Dot, a gravel-voiced mama in jeans, T-shirt and baseball cap for whom the description, "rode hard and put away wet" applied, was an endless, and I mean that in the full sense of the word, source of island lore and gossip. She'd had a full colorful life but still had a few axes to grind. She lusted after my pink and blue Miami Vice hat so I left it with her after our farewell dinner.

Five days of a rolly anchorage was enough for Chris and me. With any luck at all we'd be in Rio for Carnival. During the twenty-day passage we shared our morning coffee with Miss Phelps, who taught us rudimentary Portuguese from a Berlitz language tape. A week of moderate winds petered out to nothing so we motored southwest for two days to escape a large high-pressure system.

Half way across we sailed past an immense iron ships mooring, easily as big as TR, that had broken loose from some South American port – glad I spotted that one. We never saw a ship during our 36 days sailing in the South Atlantic until we were close to Rio. We also gave up fishing at that point due to the proliferation of plastic bags that constantly fouled our hooks.

On our approach to Rio, we sailed for a full day through a floating garbage dump. As we neared port it was accompanied by the attending smell. Regardless, the offshore view of the Sugarloaf was truly inspiring. There was so much chatter on the radio, I finally gave up trying to reach anyone in authority and sailed in to the Club Nautico where we were assigned a marina slip for the duration of our stay. I would have preferred to anchor out but it wasn't permitted.

Chris and I were really pissed at Miss Phelps when we found out she had taught us Portuguese Portuguese instead of Brazilian Portuguese, which to my ear was an entirely different language except for a few of the numbers. And don't believe anyone who says you can get by with Spanish.

Sadly, Chris's travel agent got the dates wrong for Carnival and had her return ticket booked at the beginning of festivities. We were both disappointed because we had looked forward to sharing the experience. Lucky for us, the Brazilians like to jump the gun on Carnival and we did take in a couple of neighborhood parades complete with their own samba schools before she winged her way north. Not only I, but I think the entire marina, mourned Chris's departure. The visitor's jetty wouldn't be the same without her Godiva hair and fio dental (Portuguese for dental floss, a euphemism for a Brazilian bikini).

Pickpockets all over Brazil had honed their skill to a fine art, and I'd been warned from the get-go not to walk around town with anything I wasn't prepared to lose. I quickly learned to carry my backpack against my chest and only used the deep front pockets of shorts and trousers to carry incidentals. The triple cell Maglite was also a regular companion if I planned to be out after dark.

I teamed up with Nigel, an Aussie singlehander who had just sailed around Cape Horn in a 32ft. sloop, and we took on the crowds of carnival. We alternated heavy drinking nights so one of us could keep the other out of too much trouble. The highlight came at the Sambadrome where pulsating drumbeats cranked up blood pressures in the throng of spectators and drove hundreds of near-naked sequined women into the ecstasy of dance. This was definitely not an event sponsored by the Christian Coalition. For Rio, already a teeming tropical city with its contents under pressure, the whole carnival scene acted as a giant relief valve, spewing pent-up steam into the universe. The aftermath of carnival felt as though the entire city took on the feel of a collapsed balloon.

My crew wanted notice had been up for about a week before Henk showed up. He was from Holland and had been in Rio for two years and was ready to head back north. Except for a few less years and a slightly larger frame, we looked much alike with our full beards. His fluency in Portuguese was a real plus and after five minutes I knew he'd be compatible crew. The great part was that he wanted to go all the way to Europe. Before we sailed from Rio, I contracted Pepe, a local guy to help me repaint TR's interior, a major scrape and sand undertaking. The first day went trouble free and I felt confident he knew his business. But when I returned from running an errand the second day I found four strangers crawling around TR's interior hacking away at the woodwork and Pepe sitting on deck supervising. It was obvious from the gouges in the woodwork that Pepe's "crew" was totally unskilled. Fortunately Henk was with me and we cancelled the contract in short order. I ended up doing the work myself.

A couple weeks after carnival, Henk and I sailed north toward Salvador. It took a relaxed ten days of coastal hopping and I was delighted to find Henk had a basic understanding of things nautical and an iron stomach. Winds and current were predictably contrary along this part of the coast, but the water clarity and diving made up for it. We only made one overnight passage and if it wasn't for another of my timely navigational premonitions Henk would have sailed us onto the beach. Roused at 2 a.m. for no particular reason I popped my head out the forward hatch and noticed an odd light off our starboard bow. I made my way to the cockpit snagging the binoculars off the nav table on the way. Henk, hunched under the spray dodger had no forward vision. I told him about the light and he said he'd seen it, had assumed it was a fishing boat and figured we would pass well south of it. The Fuji binoculars had great light gathering ability and when I focused on the light, there were clearly palm trees to either side of it. Guilty of similar assumptions myself on occasion, I merely handed the binocs to Henk. All he said was "OOPS". The depth sounder read 12 feet of water. We disconnected Bill and tacked. The main drawback to having a mindless crewmember like Bill is that it tends to make the mindful human on watch less observant and does nothing to enhance their helmsmanship skills. When a person is at the helm, he or she is constantly alert to the wind strength and direction, the state of the seas, performance of sails and possible hazards. But unless the watch is changed every half-hour, something like Bill will hold a far straighter course. It's all a bit of a compromise and I would rather read a book than steer all day.

Salvador, the state capital of Bahia, is another teeming tropical city but without the mountainous confines of Rio, so the humanity is spread out, not stacked up. Happily missing was that sense of impending overload. Being a major transit point for the cruising crowd, I crossed paths with a number of friends from the Indian Ocean. The surrounding cruising grounds are mostly in protected waters with numerous islands and rivers to explore. Everywhere there was evidence of working sail, from skiffs hauling building materials to the ever-present fishermen, which due to the consistency of the tradewinds made sail-power economically feasible.

This was the first time in my travels where all around town I notice posters warning people about AIDS. I hadn't a clue what AIDS was at the time but could make the connection to unprotected sex. I've never been comfortable with the idea of prostitution, always preferring to win a heart with dazzling conversation, dinner (including wine) and a movie. For someone as practically minded as myself that probably doesn't make much sense, but that's the way it is. Henk, who adores ladies of the night, filled me in on this new AIDS epidemic. It didn't take long for me to discover why Salvador was papered with warnings. Everywhere we went; petrol stations, grocery stores or bars we were propositioned. Clearly, prostitution was a major economic factor in town and I almost felt bad for not supporting it. Henk took up with a lovely mulatto woman and one time she invited us to her home. She led us to a huge multi-story open warehouse, each floor divided by assorted hanging fabrics into countless 8x8-foot cubicles, not unlike an immense temporary crafts fair. A single, bare low wattage bulb lit each cluster of four "bungalows". Hundreds of "working girls" of all ages plus their unwanted infants lived in the space and shared a communal ablution block on the first floor. A mind-dulling hubbub punctuated by shrill cries of babies permeated the place and I found myself breathing through my mouth to reduce the cloying smell. Men were only allowed as "visitors." I was afraid to ask how much the rent was. Henk's lady couldn't have been more charming and seemed oblivious to the hell around her as she somehow served us iced tea in her second story room. The next time I bump my head in TR's galley I won't be so quick to condemn my living space.

Brazilian currency was also inflating at an alarming rate. Grocery stores closed at noon so everything in the store could be re-priced for the following day. Exchange rates on the black market made kings of foreign paupers. We never went anywhere alone at night and pickpockets were constantly plying their trade especially on busses and elevators. On almost every street corner vendors would be grilling mystery meat over charcoal fires. Since there was a proliferation of cats in Salvador we called it filet meow.

In the anchorage I met Philip, a Frenchman married to a Brazilian whose father owned an emerald mine in the central mountains. We became friends and one day he brought over a tray of semiprecious gems for our consideration. He also said he could get emeralds as well. Henk bought a couple of tourmalines but I said no thanks. Several days passed before I had this absurdly romantic vision of offering emeralds to wealthy tourists in smoky bars along the south coast of France. Through Philip, a local businessman cashed my $2000 personal check (he probably owned that warehouse where all those women lived). Philip and I went to the bank for the cash. Philip was soaked in nervous sweat because our transaction could easily be witnessed through the large windows by anyone in the street. He told me people were regularly killed for $20. We came out with a large brown grocery bag stuffed with Cruzieros and tried our best not to look petrified, no cabs in sight. It was a long one-mile walk to the dinghy. That night, on his insistence, I accompanied Philip to the bus station. He wouldn't let me leave his side until he got on the bus. Ten days later, he brought me a dozen fine emeralds and I started brushing up on my French.

After six weeks we'd had too much of a good thing and headed 350 miles north to Cabadelo, a small town situated several miles up a river just past Recife, the eastern most point of Brazil. Cautious was the word when sailing along this coast. Between heavy coastal traffic, shoaling mud and large logs washed to sea by the numerous rivers we kept a sharp eye on TR's course. On our arrival we were unable to make headway against the ebbing tide and anchored temporarily at the mouth of the river. In the late afternoon we found a quiet spot a few miles upriver near a shipyard and small thatched pub. We rowed ashore for a cold beer and returned to the boat at dusk. Even though TR had never been out of our sight, someone had drifted alongside in a canoe and ransacked the boat. We'd clearly interrupted the pillage, but they still got away with plenty, as evidenced by a hastily tied bed-sheet with the stereo speakers in it and partially emptied lockers. Henk lost both his backpacks, which amounted to most of his worldly possessions. My guitar was gone as well as the basket of photographs I had of the trip to date, which, in itself, was a disaster but tucked among the many photos were the small envelopes that held the emeralds. I could just imagine the thief's disappointment at a basket full of worthless pictures and dumping the lot into the river. I lost so many odds and ends that for years afterward I would go to look for something, which I hadn't needed until that time, only to finally realize it must have been part of the missing loot. Angry, Henk and I stormed ashore and raised hell with the police. In the nearby village we posted a $100 reward (this was a lot of money for the area) for the return of our stuff. Two days later the cops took us to a small house in the village where we found one of Henk's packs with a few things still inside, the guitar case and my camera. The old man who lived there apologized for his son's behavior and wouldn't accept any reward money. The cops told us later that the man's son had pulled a gun on his father and stolen his car when his father tried to stop him. My heart really went out to the old guy. We gave it another week, hoping the guitar would show up, but the cops thought it highly unlikely. The incident (the only one of its kind in ten years) really put us off Brazil, so we scrubbed earlier plans to explore parts of the Amazon and sailed directly for the Azores, 3000 miles straight north.

Luckily I hadn't lost anything related to sailing or navigation which might have delayed our departure. We blasted out the river mouth on the falling tide into the teeth of a stiff northwest breeze. The seas were so steep TR would literally stumble off the back of each wave, plunging her bowsprit into the trough, her decks constantly awash in green water. Life below got pretty rank. Henk and I eventually moved several 80lb. pigs (cast blocks) of lead from the forward bilge into the engine room to balance the boat, a real finger smashing task only accomplished with a fountain of sweat and loud bursts of abusive language. The results kept TR's bow from diving into the wave troughs and made life tolerable. We hammered along at six knots for five continuous days without a hot meal. Then the wind shifted to the southeast and we were shoved comfortably into the doldrums.

It took five days of dodging massive thunderstorms sailing or motoring every which way but our intended course before we picked up the first breath of easterlies. During one becalmed afternoon, heat blazing in a horizonless sky, Henk and I spent four hours in tepid water plucking gooseneck barnacles from TR's bottom. It seemed as if their growth rate had reached an inch per day. We gained an extra knot of hull speed for our trouble.

I whipped up an elephant stroganoff to celebrate our equatorial crossing and we cracked our last good bottle of red wine. After a toast to Poseidon I tossed a dollop of stroganoff into the sea as a peace offering, but he must have taken exception to the cuisine. Not two seconds later we heard a loud twang and the frayed end of a ¼ inch line, that until then had held the spinner for the taffrail log, shot into the cockpit. It was another first in six years but fortunately I carried a spare.

Two thousand miles to the east there must have been one hell of a blow in the Sahara Desert, because we sailed for a full day through a gritty cloud of fine red dust. A well-timed tropical downpour saved us from hours of sluicing to rid the decks of desert sand.

After a near empty South Atlantic, the North Atlantic shipping lanes made me feel like a dog on the freeway. There were times when we had a dozen ships in sight and it seemed they were all trying to run us down. We gave up trying to fish after removing ten plastic garbage bags from the meat-hook in less than an hour.

When we finally started to pick up a radio station from the Azores I was happy to find Miss Phelps had taught me well. In fact Henk, who was fluent in Brazilian Portuguese, had to ask me for help in understanding the Slavic sounding tongue.

One rainy night, a flock of 16 sparrow-like birds took refuge on TR's deck. One brazen fowl even made itself at home in the main cabin. Our feathery freeloaders paid us no mind as we walked among them for sail changes or rigging adjustments. After a two-day rest they took off en mass to points west. Where they thought they were going was anybody's guess. Another rain shower saved us from cleaning that mess too.

Faial, like St. Helena is another gumdrop sticking out of the ocean with no off-lying dangers, but it was still a bear to find in thick fog. Twelve hours out we'd sailed into the dense white bank which screwed up my plan for visual approach to the eastern side of the island. I must have been doing something right because the first thing we picked out of the fog was the harbor breakwater at Horta, our intended landfall. A new marina had just been completed and transiting boats were obliged to take a slip. At $2 a day I couldn't complain, especially since it included water, electric and laundromat. Horta is a major stopping point for east west traffic and being far from any major landmass, all the sailors present had undertaken a substantial blue-water passage. The resulting atmosphere, minus the cocktail skippers holding forth in many marinas was, to say the least, refreshing. In keeping with tradition I painted TR's name and logo on the harbor wall among and over the thousands of other names before her.

Peter's Cafe Sport was a favorite watering hole, the upstairs of the bar dedicated to an awesome collection of scrimshaw on sperm whale teeth. Until recently the islanders had been actively whaling in sailing skiffs selecting sperm whales because they were the only whales that wouldn't sink when dead. I bought a whale's tooth from one of the locals and had a likeness of TR scrimshawed by Carlos, one of a new generation of skilled artisans. A devout catholic, Carlos exercised his artistic license and included a star-like crucifix above TR's mast – insurance for the increasingly leaky life raft.

One Sunday I rode my fold-up bike around the perimeter road, a 26-mile hilly journey that passed through a half-dozen villages. The excursion coincided with a church celebration in honor of the patron saint of the seas. I arrived at the first village just as church let out and was immediately invited to take part in the musical and feasting festivities. It so happened that there was only one priest for the entire island and services were staggered accordingly along my route. When I reached the second village the party had once again begun. This happened four more times and I was glad of the elastic band on my shorts.

During the few weeks we spent here, sailing friends from as far back as the Caribbean days passed through the marina and I caught up on all the news that was news in the cruising community. I was lucky to have Henk along since he also spoke French and German and we were certainly among an international crowd. Dockside parties were of a continuous nature, locations would change but the faces looked all too familiar. When the stories started to sound like summer re-runs, Henk and I sailed east.

Two days of fluky winds and adverse current finally got us to Sao Miguel Island where we were fortunate to meet Joao, a local sailor who took us in charge. Joao had an old Citroen and we sputtered around the island dropping into lake-filled craters and up winding, jungle-choked ravines. We swam in a volcanic hot spring that sported hot and cold waterfalls pouring in at opposite ends.

I never found it easy to depart from new/old friends as so often happens when cruising, but the mainland beckoned. Eight days of intermittent sailing and motoring brought us to Lisbon. Light winds and lumpy seas caused the mainsail to slat continuously, a necessary evil that I never learned to accept. Along the way we caught our limit of plastic bags and spent an entire afternoon sailing through a slick of waterlogged Marlboro and Winston cigarette packages complete in their cellophane wrappers. Shouldn't someone be handing out fines for littering in the shipping lanes?

We arrived in Cascais, a Lisbon suburb at 2 a.m. in a blinding squall. In a fit of protest from all that slatting, TR refused to drop her mainsail. I hoisted myself to the top of the mast to find the twelve uppermost screws on the sailtrack had backed out and jammed the slides in the track. Hey Henk, hand me that screwdriver, will ya?

July was the height of tourist season and the place crawled with pasty white Europeans and the Portuguese wisely took refuge behind their cash registers. We found that if we walked a few blocks back from the waterfront the price for a glass of wine dropped from $1.20 to 60 cents. Lisbon was my first European city and I felt as though I was walking around in a giant museum theme park. I rattled up and down the streets on the old wooded streetcars and hung out in the sidewalk cafes. Being the home of the early navigators there were a number of impressive maritime exhibits to be seen. One day Henk had stayed aboard to fix dinner while I rowed in to do a load of wash. I met a couple of nice Dutch girls and invited them back thinking Henk would be pleased to chat in his native tongue. I don't believe Henk spoke a word all through dinner and I was embarrassed for the girls. When I returned from rowing them ashore I asked Henk what the problem was. He just frowned and said, "I hate Dutch women." And that was the end of it. He took off for Holland a week later, ostensibly to earn enough money to return to Brazil in style.

Rather than look for crew this late in the season I decided to singlehand my way into the Med since the journey from here was mostly short day-hops. My ports of call along the Portuguese coast were fishing harbors. TR and I found ourselves right at home rafted to the fleet. I was never without companionship and Lord help me if I tried to pay for my own drinks. I gave away a lot of Theodora-R T-shirts.

I took advantage of the 3-meter tides on the south coast, careening TR and laying on a new coat of bottom paint. One overnighter got us to Cadiz, Spain just ahead of a dreaded Levanter, the strong east wind funneling out of the Med. Heavy swells preceded the blow when I was still four hours out and I really sweated the last few miles as the wind kept inching up the Beaufort scale and pegged at a full gale as we entered the harbor. It blew like stink for three days, but I was safely tucked away on a mooring up the river in the suburb of Jerez (sherry!).

Keeping to my priorities, I rode the train to Seville and shopped for a new guitar. I found a nice production flamenco for $100 that was a little rough on cosmetics but an otherwise bright tone and ever so easy to play. I met some friends who had brought their boat up the Guadaquivir River and were tied stern-to in front of the Club Nautico. They invited me to stay for a few days and I later sailed with them back to Cadiz. We took in a bullfight (my first) and I have to say, despite having read Hemmingway's Death in the Afternoon, I had a tough time watching those guys torment that poor bull. I even found myself cheering (bad form) when he charged one of the picador's padded horses and sent horse and rider tumbling. Leave it to an American to cheer the underdog.

Despite Seville being a big city, it had an elegant flair and a very civilized feel relative to Rio or Salvador. Sitting at a sidewalk cafe sipping a coffee, gypsy guitarists would stroll by, knock out a few bars of some wild rumba rhythm and pass the hat. I had to admire their sense of worth though, because it was a ratty hat that obviously wouldn't hold coins.

In the company of my friends from Seville, we made a dash for Gibraltar but another Levanter forced us into Barbette, a small village just shy of our destination. The wind howled for four days gusting to 80mph. On August 24th 1987 TR and I officially entered the Med, our new playground for the next few years.

Gibraltar caters to all manner of shipping traffic with great yard facilities and chandlers. Most of the yachts passing in or out of the Med stop for provisions. I swapped a good number of old charts for relevant cruising guides and charts for the Med. It was here I first heard the news of my friend Don being lost overboard in the Mozambique channel.

I hit the weekly gypsy market (flea market) to stock up on fresh produce and happened by a shoe stand when I heard the distinct sound of flamenco guitar behind the tent. I stepped around back and found two guys, one young and one old, accompanying one another to a fast Bulerias. The lady selling shoes was definitely Mom and I could tell she was terribly proud of her son's virtuosity. I stood enthralled for an hour, bought a pair of shoes I didn't really need and left inspired to pick up my new guitar.

Before heading east, I made it a point to climb The Rock and feed a bag of peanuts to the famous apes. It was an exceptionally clear day and I could easily see, across the straights, the tan and sandy countenance of Morocco – adventure beckoned.

Harbor wall Horta, Fial – Azores

Scrimshaw by Carlos

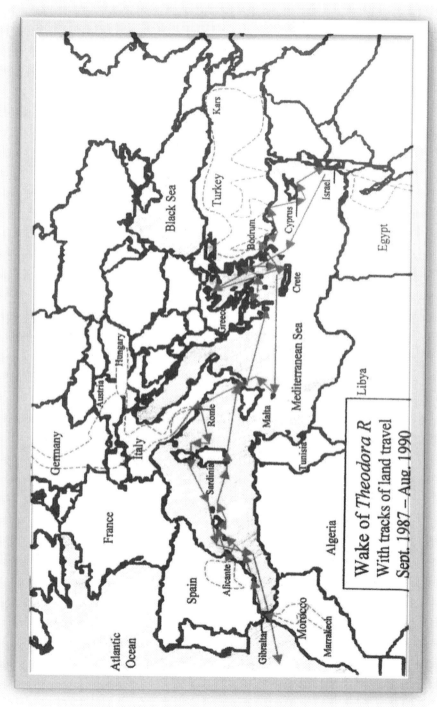

Wake of *Theodora R*
With tracks of land travel
Sept. 1987 – Aug. 1990

The Land of Ulysses

"At daybreak we were running before storm-force winds."

My sailing strategy for the Med entailed lots of motor time since the wind would either blow hard from the wrong direction or not at all. Not that there weren't some idyllic moments under pure sail, but they were rare. What my strategy didn't entail was handling a life threatening storm, a cantankerous boat spirit and a wild ride on an emotional tilt-a-whirl. My five and a half years at sea had prepared me for the first but for the rest it was definitely learn-as-you-go.

I topped up TR's tanks with cheap Gibraltar fuel and headed east, buddy boating with Hans and Liz, a German/American duo in their 40's, who were planning to winter over on Mallorca. They sailed a slick new aluminum sloop of French design, bought when the dollar was at its strongest and the Franc was at its weakest. I admired their timing and the fact that they really seemed to enjoy sailing.

Over the years I'd had an inkling that there was more to Theodora R than just a boat. Odd occurrences with no particular explanation often left me wondering. The first clear indication that TR had certain expectations of her skipper came while motoring east one evening in flat seas. Hans and Liz invited me to dinner, so, placing faith in all things mechanical, I set TR's autopilot and when they brought their boat alongside I hopped aboard. We toasted our good fortune as the two vessels ran parallel into the night. Just after I'd been handed a plate of fresh grilled tuna TR made an abrupt right turn and headed off due south. Hans changed course and chased her down so I could reset the autopilot. Nothing appeared out of order so I rejoined my friends. Not five minutes later TR again turned south. Had she gone in circles or varied her course I would have written it off to a problem with the autopilot but holding her southerly course made me think otherwise, especially since this time I remained aboard and she never again altered course.

A full moon and following breeze made for a romantic, and I use the term in the literary sense rather than the hands-on sense, approach to the Balearic Islands. At Formentera I crossed paths with several yachts that had chosen the Red Sea route out of the Indian Ocean and had just arrived from the eastern Med. We swapped yarns and after hearing about their arduous 1500 mile beat up the Red Sea, I felt I'd made the right choice going around the Cape.

My mother, Connie and sister Liz (now divorced) met me in Mallorca and we cruised the coastline for a couple weeks of good fun. Mallorca is wholesale tourism at it's best (if anything good can be said about it). During the season, the Palma airport is the busiest in Europe, bringing in a jumbo jet every 12 minutes 24 hours a day. I was impressed that the island managed to meet the needs of all those foreign travelers. The logistics of that feat alone made me shudder.

After my experience in the Seychelles the idea of wintering on a hot spot for European tourists had a definite allure, but the soul of Spanish guitar whispered in my other ear and I decided in favor of the mainland. I sailed to Alicante, a small commercial port city centrally located on the east coast. While in Mallorca I'd switched fishing tackle and now used small silver spinners with tiny treble hooks. On that 60-mile trip I hauled in 8 good-sized skipjack tuna and handed them out to other cruisers on my arrival thus accruing several future dinner invitations among the fleet.

The anchors of two dozen cruising yachts shared the harbor mud. Possessive mud it was that insured good holding when the winter storms blasted from the north. Four months later it would take me three entire days to retrieve TR's anchor, tightening the vertical chain at every low tide.

A wide paseo ringed the harbor and an old Moorish castle kept watch from high on a nearby bluff. Sunday afternoons the local symphony played music in a concert shell not a hundred yards from TR's cockpit and each evening the Spaniards would stroll arm and arm along the paseo, flaunting airs of superiority. One block back, the cobbled streets of the old city wound their way up the canyons of centuries old architecture where tapa and wine bars proliferated. Weekdays was a different story, with the cacophony of big city traffic and the periodic shriek of car alarms proclaiming the loss of another tourist's handbag or camera.

I can't tell you how often I heard the loud angry voice of the ugly American demanding an explanation as to the absence of their mail at Amex offices around the world. In compensation for this behavior, and partly for insurance, I wooed the ladies at the Amex office with flowers and never had a problem receiving mail or cashing checks.

TR got her due, the paint and varnish cans always at the ready. A local machine shop rebuilt all her fuel injectors in preparation for the expected long hours under power. I got together with a Dutchman and fellow sailor named Willem who also played Flamenco guitar. We worked up a few routines and played some evenings at a tapas bar in the old town in trade for liquid adult refreshment.

In mid February I managed a train trip to Granada and spent a cold drizzly day at the Alhambra. I was one of a dozen sightseers wandering around the ancient Moorish palace. We all got a laugh out of the signs alerting us tourists that no more than 800 persons were allowed in any of the rooms at one time. The day's low head count must have also meant a relaxed attitude in the administration office because they had the sound system cranked up playing old Elvis tunes, which pretty well squashed the imagination.

On a street below the Alhambra, I discovered luthier's row, where almost every shop heralded the name of some famous Spanish guitar maker. I spent an entire day sampling the art of many masters. I came away awed, yet delighted to learn (and this is not an unbiased opinion) that my own instruments, note for note, had a bite as bad as the big dogs.

When I returned to Alicante, fate had tossed me a tasty bone fraught with nasty splinters when chewed. She hailed from France, a dark-haired waifish gypsy with an alluring scar over one eyebrow that left her with a permanently skeptical look. Raffaella had been abandoned by her significant other who, thoughtfully, left her with their boat. Fortunately she was a handy sailor in her own right. At dockside parties we had oft times flirted in a playful way but I had never let my interest linger. But now...? One evening she rowed over for a visit and the next day rumors were rife when her dinghy was still astern. So started a yo-yo relationship that would delight and plague me throughout the Med. A word of advice for all you heartsick horny sailors out there; never, and I mean no matter how desperate the situation, share a space as small as a boat with a bipolar manic depressive. My excuse? These were the days before Prozac, and there were no telltale medication bottles lying around. Later, I would be accused of thinking with the wrong brain.

In April I set forth with two other boats, Raff on one and Mike from London on the other. We moved quickly through the Balearics to a small harbor on the western end of Menorca. TR suffered an ugly tear in her mainsail in trashy seas. Making the repair, I could see that the sail was getting a bit tired, but there were still a few years left in the Dacron.

Months earlier I had made arrangements with my friend Kim who had sailed in Africa with me, to meet in Athens in the spring. Raff and I had grown close but my departure for Greece was no surprise. A neighboring yacht had shown me a current weather fax and it looked like I had a good window all the way to Sardinia. I sailed from Menorca with tears streaming down my cheeks.

We were at 40 degrees north latitude and equinoctial storms could pounce at any time. Twelve hours later a low-pressure system that moved north out of Algeria took all thought from the kink in my heart. TR and I were soon in the grip of a full southerly gale and a critical piece of Bill's linkage broke beyond immediate repair, demanding my hand on the helm. The low intensified over the next few hours and moved further north. At daybreak we were running before storm force winds in excess of 60mph, pummeled by twenty-foot breaking seas. TR had been pushed north in the earlier gale and now we were trying to make enough southing to clear the end of Sardinia. The seas had turned ugly and it was all I could do to keep TR's stern to the bullying waves that broke into the cockpit and kept the decks awash in green water. In windless troughs the storm jib slatted unmercifully as TR rolled on her beam-ends only to snap rigid on the next crest and send a shock through the hull. I managed an awkward noon sight and found myself too far north to clear the southern point of Sardinia in the existing conditions. The tiny island of San Pietro was the only safe haven along Sardinia's rockbound coast but visibility had dwindled to a meager two miles in the airborne spindrift. I'd been at the helm for over twelve hours, running on pure adrenaline and chocolate and hoped I'd sight land before dark. The possibility of TR splintering on the rocks grew with each hour, and I was not all that optimistic about my own chances of survival especially· if things went bad in the dark. At dusk TR topped a crest and I caught a glimpse of the lighthouse on the eastern point of San Pietro. Two miles either side of that light and I would have been on the rocks. We cleared the outlying reef as the light flashed to life. Safe in the harbor, it took me several hours to get rid of the shakes. I needed four days of espresso and good pasta to rebuild Bill's linkage and my battered confidence.

I left Sardinia on a calm night for the Straights of Messina. A light northerly filled in at daylight and carried us comfortably the entire 300 miles. There were no whirlpools or Cyclopes in the straights but the cross-ferry traffic equaled any danger Ulysses encountered. I stopped briefly for fuel and fresh bread, then rounded the boot of Italy at sunset. The north wind held and TR romped across the Ionian Sea to Greece in just over two days. The entire time I single-handed in the Med I kept the half-hour beeper on my Casio watch set to the on position. Whenever I would dose off during a passage that irritating beep forced me to have a look around, which, considering the constant traffic, probably saved my bacon a few times.

TR and I tiptoed around the Peloponese peninsula, aka: little Cape Horn, but still took a thrashing rounding the central cape. We entered the Aegean with a couple weeks to kill before Kim's expected arrival in Athens.

Picture this: a crumbling stone and concrete breakwater lined with Greek fishermen, glistening strands of monofilament tying them to the sea. Beyond, a quaint harbor, blue and yellow fishing boats interspersed with the occasional foreign yacht tied stern-to to the cobbled quayside. Bordering the harbor, a row of upscale trendy shops that only open when the cruise-ships disgorge their colorful human cargo draped in cameras. Rising from the harbor basin, banks of whitewashed interlocking cubes topped with terracotta tile divided by the dark veins of steep stone stairways. Royal-blue trim frames the windows and ancient wooden doors, invariably accented with red geraniums. The odd cat sleeps on the windowsill and donkeys bray from hidden alleyways. Stretching to the impossible cobalt sky are the dusky, near-barren peaks crisscrossed with low rock walls and goat trails. A hot, dry downdraft, the breath of Greece, is laced with sage, garlic and oregano mixed with a hint of barnyard. This, in a nutshell, is my impression of cruising the islands of Greece, all a slight variation on the above theme. The islands are scattered about the Aegean in such a way that each afternoon I would be anchored in a different harbor, seated in the sun at a whitewashed waterfront tavern relaxing with my chilled retsina, bread and fried octopus. As cruising grounds go, one could certainly do worse.

In Piraeus harbor, rafted to an abandoned fishing boat, I had an unobstructed view of the Parthenon, which, despite its proximity, was merely a blurred impression in the smog of Athens. In a wide bay beyond the breakwater the mothballed fleets of forgotten Greek shipping tycoons quietly surrendered to rust. The breakwater, a favorite party spot for car-obsessed teens reverberated with pop music until 4 a.m. daily. It would be a short stay. I met Kim at the airport and knew immediately something was amiss. Prying inquiries brought forth tears and the regretful separation from her lover's arms ten hours ago. This was not unlike my own situation with Raffaella but I'd had a month to get over it. She departed for home with my blessing and I got the hell out of Athens.

I put in to Paros to think things over and take care of some neglected varnish work. After a few phone calls and several days wait, I spoke with Raffaella. She was in Malta and wanted help bringing her own boat to Greece. I had no desire to sail back 400 miles and have two vessels to deal with, but again fate intervened. Not two hours after I had spoken with Raff, my friends Phil and Monica, British cruisers who I'd met when I first arrived in Greek waters, tied up their 40-foot gaff-rigged cutter next to TR. That evening, over sundowners in their cockpit I told them of my quandary. They broke out laughing. Turns out they had wanted to sail to Malta but had put it off because they wanted extra crew for the trip.

I left TR under the watchful eye of a local tavern owner and a week later I was in the outskirts of Valletta picking wild capers with Raff, and a great reunion it was. Phil and Monica had made a good call wanting extra crew for the Malta trip, because we hand-steered downwind in a raging gale for three days.

Raff's boat, Manahiki was only a 28-foot sloop, her sails and rigging felt like toys to me. We sailed for Greece and ran out of wind within 24 hours. Maybe it was the drone of the two-cylinder diesel or the endless flat horizon, but for the first time I witnessed Raff fall off an emotional cliff. Five knots is just not fast enough when you need to get off a boat. It seemed I could do nothing to staunch the tears or wild ravings, so I huddled in the cockpit, hand on the tiller, aiming for the closest land. Eventually the rumbles from the cabin subsided and sleep took charge. At dawn a loud clanking came from the engine room. I lifted the hatch and saw instantly that the engine had vibrated loose from its mounts. Highly motivated, I worked like a man possessed to secure the iron beast, lashing this, wedging that and coaxing new life from the old engine mounts. The smell of espresso from the galley brought my work to a halt. I peeked below just as a smiling Raffaella handed me a cup of steaming brew. It appeared that she and the motor both were back on an even keel. That night we anchored on the Peloponese peninsula and I no longer felt the need to abandon ship. As we cruised north to pick up TR the romantic veil once again covered my eyes and Raff and I settled into the routine of togetherness.

Wide splits in the planking of TR's foredeck indicated her displeasure at being left alone. She had definitely suffered worse sun exposure than here over the years and she really had no excuse. I told her, in no uncertain terms, that she would have to get over it. Exasperated, I spent a morning on my knees, caulking-iron in hand tapping home new cotton until it rang, then repainted the offended area.

Raff had gone for a walk, returning in a blue mood that soon turned black and ugly. She told me she no longer wanted my company and made preparations to leave port. Nothing I said made a difference and, totally confused, I watched her sail off.

The next day I moved to Hydra, where I'd made good friends ashore, and drank the lady off my mind. The crew wanted sign went up and in no time I'd signed on a couple of young bucks in the midst of a post-graduation backpacking tour. All the short hops and fluky winds made for a lot of strenuous activity aboard and I gladly delegated those chores to them. We made a couple forays around Hydra to acquaint the crew to TR's many quirks. The day before our planned departure for islands in the central Aegean, Raffaella appeared at TR's stern with two large duffel bags looking lost and forlorn. Jesus, I thought, now what?

Seems her ex wanted his boat back and had the Greek police impound it. Homeless, she'd tracked me down to throw herself on my mercy. She, of course, was her most charming self, casting spells, wooing my new crew and, I hate to admit it, me into the bargain.

TR, with a compliment of four, sailed north with honeybee random, choosing destinations at the whim of the wind or lack thereof. On the practical side, we were never charged harbor fees, paying only for water. But it seemed as though every chunk of hand carved rubble posing as "Greek Ruins" had a price. We soon learned to keep our distance, because up close there was so much concrete reconstruction at these sites that it diminished the whole, making distant impressions far superior. Fishing seemed pointless after days of nary a bite. Taking the advice of local fishermen, I took to spearing octopus, who gave away their presence by the Zen garden of discarded shells at their doorstep. Once introduced to the pressure-cooker their tough muscle turned soft as marshmallow and became a staple aboard TR. Eventually, the old wizened eyes of these incredibly intelligent creatures would see through to my inner soul and convince me to remove them from the menu. They became my friends, entertaining me for hours with their coy come-hither games.

A month later, my two strapping lads left us in Lesbos to take advantage of the last week of their Eurail pass. My back and biceps were sorry to see them go. Unexpectedly, my stepbrother Don showed up on the quay. The cruise-ship he worked on was in port for repairs and he happened to be on holiday. I hadn't seen Don for nearly ten years and it was great to catch up on our lives.

We set out to circumnavigate Lesbos and met Simone, an 80-year-old goatherd who taught us a lesson. One afternoon we'd been carefully picking apples from the branches of what we assumed was a wild unattended tree when in the distance we heard a shout. An ancient man, arms waving, came hollering down the hillside. Busted, we were prepared to surrender our forbidden apples. The guy came up sputtering what I was sure were Greek expletives of the vilest sort and motioned us away from under the tree. He then climbed with astounding alacrity into the higher branches, grabbed hold of the main trunk and shook the beejeezus out of the tree. Apples rained down and we had to jump further back to avoid being clobbered. He hopped down and even though he said it in Greek his motions clearly said, "That, is how you pick apples."

A day later he butchered a goat, grilled it on a spit and had us and his family of ten over for a feast. Seated at a long planked table in front of his modest house of plywood and tin, we gorged ourselves on unknown delicacies prepared by his extended family. When the meal ended we made motions to clean up, but Simone waved us off and proceeded to toss all the ceramic plates down the hillside where, smashed to shards, they joined a growing heap of past sacrifices. That, is how you do dishes.

Raff and I left Don on Lesbos and sailed across the channel to Turkey. We cleared in at Ayvalik, where although the paperwork was a bit confusing, the officials couldn't have been more pleasant. In fact, at first I thought it was all an act, being offered tea and a comfortable chair. I expected the ax to fall in the form of some exorbitant clearance fees or some such thing. But no, it turns out they were honestly pleased to see us and welcome us to their country. As I walked back to the boat I couldn't help thinking, what is so difficult about being pleasant that most places I'd been in and out of can't seem to get a handle on it?

Turkey was my first Moslem country and I was acutely aware of the subservient role women play in this society. Even Raff felt compelled to wear long trousers and basically cover up which was not her normal state. We were both enchanted by the mosques and the muezzin calling the faithful to prayer. We cruised south well away from the tourist trail. In one secluded bay we found bathtub size hot springs along the water's edge, front-ring seats for a major thunderstorm that rolled in from Greece.

In Eskifocha, a resort for Turks on holiday, we tied stern-to in front of a newly opened pastry shop. The owners, several young professionals, dentists, lawyers and a physician, wanted something to do in their spare time. After a few days, TR was as much a home to them as the shop was to us. We took excursions to their favorite beaches and TR was never short on pastries or good Turkish coffee.

Reluctantly we cast off for points south and maybe it was all the sugar in our recent diet, but Raff went into another death spin as we neared Sigachek. Fortunately we were soon in harbor and I could step ashore. The following day, at Raff's suggestion, I put her on the bus to Izmir and from there she flew home to Paris. Again I'd been lulled into complacency and become attached, but another side of me toasted her departure with relief. She knew my general itinerary, but I didn't really expect her to return.

In Chesme I found a forgotten love and TR expressed her displeasure by flooding her bilge from an unknown source. After anchoring in the well-protected harbor, I secured the companionway hatch and rowed ashore without bothering with sail covers as it was already late in the day. This was my first town where tourism was king and I became dazzled by the displays of fine textiles. Vibrant wool carpets, kilims whose intricate designs beckoned with mystery and the exotic silk rugs from Hereke all conspired to tantalize me. My love of textiles was violently reawakened. I couldn't get enough.

Achmet, a trim middle aged Turk with a thin dark mustache took me under his wing. I was a willing student and he shared my passion for textiles. Sunk in the embroidered cushions of his shop, we drank endless cups of tea while he educated me to the subtleties of Gordian knots, natural dyes and true antiques. And the smell, that wholesome earthiness of wool. A new world opened before me. I returned to TR at dawn, climbed below and stepped into an inch of water. My first thought was, Oh, you bitch. But out loud I asked, "Okay, what is it now?" Luckily the bilge pump responded with a healthy hum when I flicked the switch and I heard water being returned to the harbor where it belonged. A thorough search uncovered no clue as to the point of entry. I could almost see her then, Theodora Regina, co-ruler of Rome with Justinian in 400A.D. aka: The Whore of Babylon. She eyed me with that haughty, malicious look of a stunning woman who screwed her way to the throne, countless corpses in her wake. As a saving grace, and this applies in particular to her nautical namesake on whom I depend, she is a survivor. I winked at the image and hit the sack.

As I cruised south to Kushadasi, Didim, and Selchuk, I found willing mentors. Soon I knew at a glance the origin of a certain piece or whether the dyes were aniline or natural. I could feel the quality of a new carpet in the tightness of its weave, spot flaws by looking at the backside where mistakes are easily seen. I recognized the different flatweave techniques, sumak, gigim and zili. I was in awe of the one million hand-tied knots needed in each square meter of a silk carpet from Hereke. I had it bad, the rug bug.

In fitful winds that called for constant sail changes and adjustment, I finally fired up the iron genny and motored the last 30 miles to Bodrum, our planned winter headquarters. Guarded by the intimidating stone battlements of an ancient Crusader's castle, now an archeology museum of the highest order, Bodrum harbor was a snug enclosure due to a recent extension of the breakwater. Twenty other foreign yachts swung at anchor, waiting for the last of the tourist vessels to be dry-docked, thus vacating the quayside for the winter. Just as I dropped anchor half a dozen mosques surrounding the harbor sang out with their call to prayer. I took it as a welcome sign. I stood on TR's foredeck surveying the harbor basin, white stucco rising into the hills. My eye caught on at least five carpet shops. This, I thought, could be heaven.

The clatter of oars being shipped brought me out of my reverie. A Dutch accent yelled, "Have a package for you." In the stern of the dinghy was a cute brunette with short hair. The hair threw me and for a moment I didn't recognize Raffaella. She followed her duffle aboard and waved goodbye to her ride. I stood mute in emotional fireworks. I returned her hug and managed a shaky, "Welcome back." Enchanted as I was with her cheery side, I knew

Mrs. Hyde lurked below and I didn't want to contend with her.

I was gun shy and for several days kept a wary eye out for a telltale dark cloud. A timely visit by my mother, Connie and her friend Mary got us off the boat for a few weeks of bus and train travel around central Turkey. From the soft ice cream cone landscapes of Cappadocia to the Hitite museum in Ankara and carpet shops of Konya, we were constantly on the move, pausing mostly to savor the vegetable-rich delicacies of Turkish cuisine. Connie loved to shop and Raff was only too happy to help, leaving me free to continue work on my textile degree. However, I kept waiting for the inevitable crack in Raff's veneer. It didn't show up until we got back to Bodrum. Maybe the cessation of constant activity set her off, who knows. Even though I was mentally prepared for it, the scene still freaked me out. I couldn't take it anymore, so, when she left the boat for the afternoon, I moved her stuff into a hotel ashore. The tantrum on her return was easy to take knowing I would no longer have to live with it. She eventually settled into her new digs and I sailed to a quiet cove down the coast for a week of R and R. On my return she was gone.

Each Wednesday the market came to Bodrum, lining the quayside with stand after stand of produce, olives, meat, honey, shoes, coats, and hardware. I would have to watch my step leaving the boat so I didn't trip over a box of farm eggs or stomp on an eggplant. $5 would fill TR's larder for the week, so there was plenty left over to sample Turkish wines and Greek brandy. Did I say sample? I think 'indulge in' would be more appropriate. My immediate neighbors on one side were Dutch and on the other, Danish. The common language among the fleet was English but I was able to practice my Turkish in the carpet shops.

Where I was going with my obsession with carpets and kilims I didn't know. I hadn't bought anything yet and wanted to know more before I made a purchase. I had spent enough time in the shops to know that all rug dealers are storytellers or more aptly put, total bullshitters. One of my favorite "sales tools" was the small innocuous sign posted next to a prominently displayed piece that read 'Private Collection – not for sale'. It was amazing how desirable the piece would become when it was no longer available. More than once I witnessed a reversal in the rules of bargaining when a customer upped the ante until the dealer could no longer "refuse" the sale. It reminded me of an old country tune whose lyrics go, "I learned something I'll never forget, women like men that they can't get."

About mid November I organized my 38th birthday celebration aboard TR and scoured the Wednesday market for special cheeses, olives and dessert treats. At one stall selling marzipan I was intrigued by a tall attractive woman in a gray overcoat, clearly a foreigner, who was bargaining in fluent Turkish with a slight German accent. She got her marzipan for a good price so I indicated to the seller I wanted a kilo of the same. One thing led to another and I learned the German lady's name was Anna and she was on an extended holiday. Now, for all you boat owners out there if you ever need a good line try, "I'm having a birthday party aboard my yacht tonight, would you like to come?"

Imagine my delight when later I found that Anna shared my passion for textiles and was well aquatinted with a number of the carpet dealers in and around Bodrum. Soon we were inseparable, making forays to the mountain villages in the vicinity where the regional Milas carpets are made.

An unexpected windfall of cash came when the people I'd sold some property to years ago paid off the note I still held. This, more than anything, led to my decision to invest in kilims for later sale in the states. I chose kilims for three reasons, 1-lighter weight – carpets weigh a ton, 2-they fold into relatively small bundles for easy storage aboard, and 3- less expensive as a general rule. Armed with a working knowledge of the trade and the financial means, Anna and I made plans to scour the weaving centers of central and eastern Turkey.

Winter storms could turn a serene place like Bodrum Harbor into a huge washing machine stuck on the agitation cycle when bullets of wind roared out of the hills. I set TR's two big anchors, the 65lb plow and the 60lb Danforth, which kept her safely away from the quay when things got hairy. My neighbors promised to keep an eye on TR while I traveled inland and I warned them of her spiteful trick, flooding the bilge.

The downside of winter travel in Turkey was the incessant cigarette smoke on busses with their windows now shut tight and the chewable smog in the towns where they burned coal for heat. Anna and I were both ex-smokers addicted to fresh air, so chasing after winter deals on rugs in these condition was a true test of our resolve. We coughed our way from town to town, shop to shop, convincing ourselves with each special find that lung disease was a fair trade for some really spectacular textiles. And just to impress upon you what gung-ho rug warriors we were, almost all Turkish rug dealers are chain smokers and in the winter the shop doors are closed.

Our travels took us north and east as far as Kars, where we made an excursion to the ancient ruins of Ani. The 80-foot tall minaret, a lone sentinel jutted from the rubble of a thousand year old mosque. Worn stone steps spiraled up into the darkness, a dare I couldn't pass up. Besides, there were no signs that read "do not enter." From the top I could easily see across the river into Russia where several guard towers spoke of the iron curtain.

On the bus south, skirting the snowcapped peak of Mount Ararat, we met Paul, an athletic balding lawyer from Santa Fe, who was on holiday. We hit it off and he traveled with us for a week or so. Before he departed, he promised to meet us in Portugal the following fall and crew with us across the North Atlantic.

As our collection of rugs grew, we would periodically send a bundle on the bus back to a friend's carpet shop in Bodrum or to Konya where expert repairs could be made to damaged or worn pieces. Most of the kilims we bought were an average age of fifty years and we chose them for their dye quality and designs. Turks don't consider anything less than 200 years old true antiques and those were most likely in museums. Newer kilims were now being made for the tourist trade but these pieces, although nicely made, lacked the spirit of the older kilims that had been made for the personal use of the weaver or their family. As the families needed money, these rugs would trickle into local carpet shops and that's where we found them.

Van, Diyabakir, Adana, Kaysari, Gaziantep, were exotic place names on our textile trail and one by one we came to know them. Some places we would return to years later as our rug business evolved into more than a hobby. But travel in the southeast had its hazards. Because of Kurdish rebels military roadblocks held up our busses for hours at a time. I figured if I was a Kurdish rebel intent on kidnapping a foreigner to use as a bargaining chip, I'd be watching the roadblocks where the busses are already stopped and everyone was wandering around outside.

TR's waterline settled some as the bundles of rugs took up more and more space. Sail bags were soon relegated topside and lashed to the cabin top. The whole boat now smelled of damp wool. As spring blossomed in the countryside we pulled up the two muddy anchors and slowly coastal hopped eastward, our sights set on Israel.

Carpet Market – Yahila, Turkey

Bodrum Harbor from the castle ramparts

Per and me building a dinghy

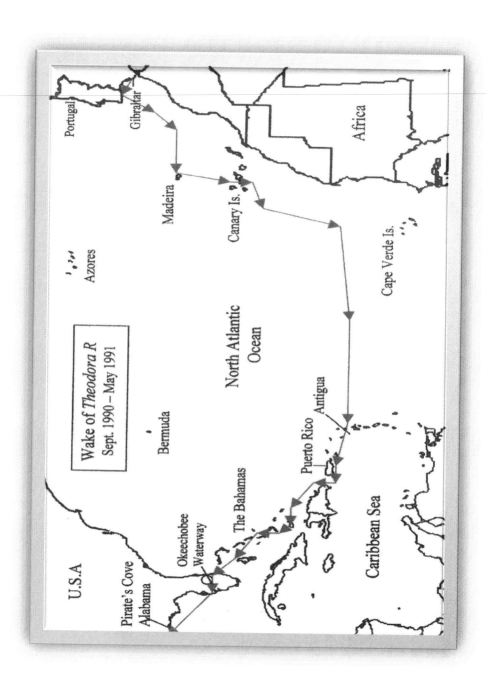

Wake of *Theodora R*
Sept. 1990 – May 1991

The Eastern Med and the Atlantic

"Relax, won't get worse than that."

The Danish couple, Per and Jette, who had been our neighbors for the winter of '88, sailed in tandem with us for several weeks along the south coast of Turkey. I had helped Per build a replica of TR's dinghy with a few modifications so it would fit on the foredeck of Nausicaa, a sleek wooden forty-foot yawl. The project had been an exercise in patience for me because I tend to shoot from the hip and eyeball even the most critical measurement, but not Per. Out came the tape measures and calipers and a project that could have taken 3 days took a week. But what the hell, it wasn't like we were on a tight schedule. We had shared many a meal over the winter and put away a cask or two of good Rhodes brandy. One evening in a quiet anchorage near Kas, they hailed us to come celebrate. "Celebrate what?" I asked when we rowed over.

"The fall of the Berlin Wall."

Where Per had found a cold magnum of champagne I'll never know, as I was sure we had drunk up everything aboard our respective vessels by then. We listened to live reports on the BBC of what would certainly be the most significant global development during my ten-year cruise. Anna, being German, was especially touched. I no longer thought of myself as an American but rather a citizen of the world and dismantling the wall I considered a big step in the right direction for the mindset of mankind in general.

My two blonde sisters Carla and Liz joined us for the trip to Israel, showing up in Kas with an armload of rugs, the result of taking refuge in a carpet shop during a rainstorm. Per and Jette couldn't make up their collective minds about joining us and we left them muddled in indecision as we sailed for Cyprus. The first day passed pleasantly enough but we got trounced by severe thunderstorms the next. Gusty squalls hammered TR and she suffered another blown seam in her mainsail. Fortunately we were able to reef past the tear and still use the sail. Carla and Liz were in the land of the living dead and would later refer to the trip as the "Passage from Hell." Lightening struck in blinding bolts the night through and TR's rigging glowed green with St. Elmo's fire. The marina in Larnaca, when we'd cleared the breakwater, looked pretty good to the crew.

Cyprus has the distinction of being the only place I encountered requiring a photo taken on arrival. It seemed they were building dossiers on all transient residents. After a few days in recovery and repairing the mainsail, we ventured forth. A light northeast breeze took pity on us and gave us a 36-hour dream sail to Tel Aviv. As we approached the coast at midnight I kept calling the Israeli defense force on channel 16 with no results. Soon I became aware of a low rumble from astern. I could see nothing in the moonless night. Suddenly, daylight struck, blinding us under the intense beam of an arc light. A booming loudhailer asked our intentions. I established radio contact and we ultimately satisfied the defense force of our innocence. After asking our intended landfall, they wished a pleasant stay, never hinting that we were expected to wait until daylight to enter the harbor in Tel Aviv. We crept in at 4 a.m. and tied to the visitor's jetty.

Insistent knocking on TR's deck roused us at 6:30. I poked my head from the forward hatch and met the angry verbal onslaught of an armed guard dressed in military fatigues. It was clear a boatload of foreigners had slipped in under his nose and his bluster was to cover his embarrassment. First Carla, then Liz followed by Anna, all sporting sleep-tossed hair, dragged themselves up the companionway and into the cockpit, squinting in the daylight. The guard, silenced by the sight of my harem couldn't keep a straight face and was soon shaking his head as he went to bring us a pot of fresh coffee. TR was given a slip from a traveling member of the yacht club and we felt free to travel around.

The Arab moneychangers in Jerusalem gave us the best exchange on dollars for shekels and we found a few rare bargains in the rug shops of the old city. We obtained visas for Egypt and took the overnight bus to Cairo, a military escort all the way. A month earlier the bus had been attacked and several tourists killed by machine-gun fire. No, I did not sleep on the bus ride.

The Arab experience was intense, leaving my mind a numb blob after two weeks of wanderings down the Nile Valley on the train to Luxor and back through Dahab on the Red Sea. Every transaction needed sharp bargaining skills that we had not grown up with so mental fatigue set in usually at the most critical point leaving us feeling like we'd been had once again. Toward the end, and much to their astonishment, I even gave vendors their asking price. But hey, I'll never forget riding camels around the great pyramids, the sunrise over Abu Simbal, trekking into the Valley of the Kings or the great temples of Luxor. I'd always heard about the awesome diving in the Red Sea and can now say it is exquisite. Carla and Liz left us in Luxor, taking a Nile cruise back to Cairo and home. Anna and I spent our last night in Dahab curled under a wretched smelly camel blanket in a dilapidated plywood storage shed that had been billed as mid-range accommodation. But it only cost 50 cents and kept the mosquitoes out. I had to admire the young Aussies and Americans that had been on the road for years living out of their backpacks. I missed TR.

At the Israeli border we collapsed in the luxury of an air-conditioned bus. But as we neared the Dead Sea, most of the passengers had gotten off and there was only one young woman and the obligatory armed soldier up front with the driver. As a way of stacking the odds in my favor in the event of a possible accident, I always sat halfway back on the right (assuming right hand driving). My eye rested on a lone bundle, seemingly abandoned, under a seat up the aisle from ours. I nudged Anna and pointed it out. We looked at each other and scrambled toward the front. The driver pulled over immediately and we all clattered off, except the poor soldier who went back to investigate. Two tense minutes ticked by and he finally appeared grinning. It was a sack full of figs.

We changed busses at the Dead Sea and the layover gave me plenty of time for a swim and a quick look around for the odd scroll. Entering Tel Aviv I noticed with pleasure the total absence of blaring car horns. TR must have felt well looked after since she exhibited no outward sign of discontent. In fact I think she was just as ready to leave that bizarre state of affairs called the Middle East as we were because she motored three entire days back to Turkey in flat seas without a hitch.

We stopped in Rhodes and met Per and Jette who were there with the same intent. Bearing empty jugs the four of us took the well-worn path to the brandy distillery. I believe TR may have been unhappy about my drinking habits of late because we found her well flooded, canned goods and carpeting afloat, on our return. Had we decided to stop for a meal out she may well have sunk herself in the harbor. The bilge pump worked hard for an hour before I could see a jet of water coming in from the stern gland where the prop shaft passed through the hull. It hadn't been leaking when we'd left the boat.

By the time we left Turkey and began our journey west to Gibraltar, there were over fifty kilims aboard, leaving scant space for our usual horde of stores. On occasion I would recall the lost emeralds and think how that same investment fit easily in one hand. At a gusty anchorage in Greece I helped an older couple anchor their powerboat when conditions made the task unwieldy for just the two of them. Over cocktails later I told of my travels and when I got to the part about the emeralds the lady broke in, "Oh, do you have any with you? I love emeralds" – Rats.

In Panomitas Bay the worlds tastiest bread could be found at the monastery where an order of elderly nuns bake it daily. Here I salvaged a large bronze propeller and the stainless prop shaft from an old sunken fishing boat. The combined weight of these two items was over a thousand pounds. The prop, securely lashed to the cabin top, would maybe make a nice coffee table one day. The shaft? Well, that I later floated ashore in Gibraltar with a dozen boat fenders and sold it to a scrap yard for $150 – not bad for five days of hard work.

Near Kithira we spotted a 60-foot fin whale, an unusual sight especially for the Med.

Sailing north from the Straights of Messina we passed the volcanic cone of Stromboli during an overcast night. The rosy reflection of the lava-filled crater pulsated like a dragons breath on the cloud-cover, a beacon to mariners for centuries.

In Rome, a small shipyard up the Tiber river agreed to watch over TR when Connie and another friend, Rose, flew in for a car tour of central Europe. I hadn't driven a car since I'd been in South Africa so you can imagine my stress level driving in Rome. I managed to get hopelessly lost trying to find our way out of the city, becoming a total basket-case. I believe from a situation like this lie the roots of the phrase, "cuss like a sailor". I turned the driving over to Anna and took over navigation. Finally, a system that worked. The following itinerary can be sung to the tune of Route 66: Florence, Venice, Zagreb, Budapest, don't forget Vienna, Munich, Worms, Grindelwald, Genoa. Get your kicks on.... It was the kind of trip that makes your eyes glaze over but all the classics like Michaelangelo's David, the Leaning Tower and the north face of the Eiger made an impression. A traveling European folk dance group highlighted one memorable stay at a refurbished castle outside Vienna. At precisely 4 p.m. a hundred costumed dancers and musicians piled out of three busses, performed outrageously for three hours on the manicured grounds then magically vanished in a cloud of diesel exhaust.

The drive through northern Italy on our return to Rome, the steep winding roads, olive groves and vineyards adorning the hillsides, was a dreamy time – probably because we could rarely drive over 15 mph.

Through friends of friends we sold our first kilims to an Italian couple who braved the wool dust in the confines of TR's cabin. Showing large rugs on a small boat is especially awkward for someone who had become a lazy sailor. The harsh reality of physical labor mad me rue even more the loss of those emeralds.

A month in river water had left TR's hull below the waterline spotless, which probably went a long way to appease TR's pique at being left alone. She seemed to have no complaint as we set forth for Corsica. The winds forced us into Porto Chervo on the north end of Sardinia, playground of the rich and famous. TR was by far the saltiest of ships among that crowd.

Three hundred-foot sheer white cliffs protected the deep all-weather harbor of Bonifacio, at the south end of Corsica. I could easily imagine Napoleon's fleet hiding out here. Touring was out of the question because moped rentals started at $110 a day. I didn't even ask about cars.

Back in Menorca, we hung out in Mahone for over a month attending to the Queen, lavishing her with new paint and varnish. As soon as the Italians went on vacation, our quiet anchorage, shared with two other cruising yachts, was literally bumper to bumper with massive ten-boat raft-ups where boisterous parties raged through the night. One nice thing about living on a boat is if you don't like your neighbors, you can move.

The American Navy, bristling with implements of war, had maxed out all available parking in Gibraltar. Trend setting tan-cammo paint jobs cleverly disguised every piece of deck cargo in preparation for Desert Storm. The vibes seemed to alter the flow of good energy in the universe. We didn't linger, sailing within two days for Tangier.

The fenced harbor under 24-hour military guard seemed as good a place as any to leave TR while we undertook a train ride to the interior. After a couple forays into the marketplace of Tangier we knew what we were up against and girded ourselves for two weeks of hard bargaining. The inevitable pipe of hashish floating around the teahouses helped take the edge off.

Like a cross between Disney World and some destitute slum, the souks (markets) in Fes and Marrakesch lived up to all the rumors. From snake charmers and dancing bears to blind multiple amputees begging in pitiful rags. All is available for a price. Need some Spanish fly? Rhino horn? A hit man? You got it. We were looking for kilims and weren't disappointed. The radical mix of pungent odors sent our heads into a spin. Our biggest problem was keeping our selection to a manageable quantity. I could have filled a cargo container.

Anna and I were both suckers for street food and paid the price with a killer bout of the Moroccan Munge in Fes. Never in my travels had I been so ill. Talk about pungent odors! We found refuge in a small hotel near the souk with a lovely inner courtyard that we were in no shape to really appreciate. But the lush tropical landscaping did wonders for filtering out the incessant noise of the city. I think the peace and quiet did more to speed our recovery than anything else. Somehow four days passed without notice except for the heartfelt kindness shown by the proprietor and his sweet wife.

Loaded with two giant sacks full of rugs we muscled our way aboard the train in Marrakech and found a near empty compartment where we could stretch out on the wooded bench. I hadn't realized the train originated there, so after the third stop heading toward Tangier we were perched on our bundles, elbow to painful elbow with humanity. Even the overhead luggage racks held inert bodies, legs and arms adangle.

How we managed to stuff this last load of kilims aboard TR is a mystery − talk about cramming fifty pounds into a thirty-pound sack! Somewhat low on her waterline, TR waddled out of Tangier and punched through lumpy seas towards Portugal. A cursory stop by the Spanish Coast Guard to see how much hashish we were smuggling slowed our passage down by several hours. Next time I'll say <u>carpet</u> dealer not <u>rug</u> dealer.

As promised, Paul, our transatlantic crew member, met us in Faro, Portugal. We spent a few days provisioning and gave TR's bottom a good scrubbing. I could almost hear her giggle. A rigging problem at the masthead made us miss a slack tide departure (was that a chuckle I heard coming from TR's bilge?) Consequently, when we left the lagoon the overfalls, where outgoing tide met the sea, had grown to six feet plus. TR has a bluff bow but we still submarined through that wall of water. Decks awash, cockpit flooded, TR gave the new crew a good scare. I told Paul, "Relax, won't get worse than that." He was skeptical.

After a short stint of motoring, the wind filled from the north and we had a comfortable sail all the way to Madeira. It proved to be one of the most pleasant passages in nine years at sea. The rolly anchorage in Funchal encouraged us to spend the days ashore playing mountain goat and tasting wine. I don't believe there is a flat road anywhere on the island. We had sailed from Portugal with a dry boat to give my liver a break, but couldn't pass up some fine Madeira from Madeira. This would all be gone by the time we left the Canaries and I'd be suitably dried out and prepared for the ever-present rum bottle in the Caribbean. I have to say, of all things social in the cruising community, drinking is almost a given, cocktails a standard preface to any visit. There were times when I had to consciously work at retarding the pickling of my liver. Every port of call had its share of rummy sailors who survived on lobster found beneath the coral heads growing from the bottoms of their boats. There were times I had come close falling into that trap, but luckily I'm one of those people who really dislikes drinking in the daytime.

A mistake in navigation (mine by making an assumption) brought us to the island of La Palma instead of Tenerife. No matter, there was deep water right to shore and I had my bearings before we made landfall. We had to row through 3-foot breakers to land on the beach. Anna and Paul sat in the stern while I rowed. We surfed in and I felt the bow touch sand. At my order they jumped out before we were swamped by the next wave. But there was no beach at the stern and they both disappeared in the foam. I stepped calmly into ankle deep water. When Paul came sputtering ashore I burst out laughing. His T-shirt read QUESTION AUTHORITY.

An all day hike around the rim of the extinct crater on La Palma easily made up for missing Tenerife. The spectacular flowering jungle and sheer black cliffs plunging hundreds of feet were beyond words. We had no desire to hang out so after lugging aboard a fifty-pound stalk of bananas we sailed for Hierro, our last stop before crossing the Atlantic. What appeared to be a snug harbor on the south end turned into a hell-hole when the North Atlantic swells rolled in. TR was like a tethered bull in the chute, bellowing whenever she brought her 15 tons up hard on her docklines. The protest of overstressed lines kept us awake all night. At 4 a.m. when the first line snapped, I had the crew prepare for first-light departure. There were no supplies we needed bad enough to hang out here longer than absolutely necessary. We didn't even bother to clear out.

Light westerlies pushed us south for several days and we started looking at charts for the Cape Verde Islands. But near the Tropic of Cancer the northeast trades kicked in and we laid our course west with an escort of a dozen pilot whales. In mid-Atlantic the winds ceased on my birthday, November 14th. TR sat quietly on a motionless sea. The temperature rose and we went for a dip. Paul had the misfortune to kiss the near-invisible tentacle of a jellyfish masquerading as a plastic bag. His lips swelled to a state of pucker that would qualify him for a 900 phone ad.

The next day we were below playing cards and at noon I climbed topside with the sextant to check our latitude. I gave the horizon a cursory look and my bowels turned to liquid. North of us, stretching east to west as far as I could see was a black sausage-shaped cloud. Dangling, like the undulating arms of a giant octopus, were eight evil-looking waterspouts. These are tornadoes at sea packing winds over 200 mph. They were close enough that I could see the whirling white water on the surface of the sea. I called all hands and we stared in horrified fascination at the spectacle. As we watched, one spout was sucked back into the cloud and further along two more dropped down – a monster quenching its thirst. I finally snapped out of it and fired up the diesel, making a lightening fast getaway at 5 knots. We stripped the deck of all moveable objects and put extra lashings on everything else. As we lumbered to the southwest during the afternoon a total of 22 spouts touched down. One passed less than a mile from our stern. By dusk they had all dissipated and a fresh breeze filled in from the north. With sails up I made like a sheepherder and got the flock outta there.

Light to moderate winds took us the rest of the way. The night before we reached Antigua, a Russian freighter appeared from astern, red and green nav lights visible and white lights in line – collision course. I got on the radio and eventually got a response, "Yes, we see you." But they did not alter course. Soon their bow loomed from the darkness, I veered to starboard and the bastard passed 100 feet to port. The crew lined the well-lit deck all waving like maniacs. We mooned 'em.

I hove-to for half the night and reached into Falmouth harbor at daybreak, tying the knot on my circumnavigation at 0700 on November 28th 1990 – party time.

And yes, I felt pretty good about accomplishing something I'd set out to do, the least of which was to sail around the globe. I came away with a much more objective view of world affairs and an inside look at how the rest of the world viewed America. Network news would never be the same.

Paul flew back to being an attorney in Santa Fe, and as a treat to TR I ordered a new suit of tanbark sails from Lee Sails in Hong Kong. Anna had taken to the cruising life with the attention to detail that only Teutonic bloodlines could appreciate. I will always be a lazy sailor and therein lay a working relationship.

One of our first encounters ashore turned out to be with Marcus, my old crew from the Indian Ocean. He was there with his thirty-footer which had gotten clobbered by a hurricane the previous year and now needed extensive repair. He'd assimilated well into the Antigua yachting scene and even wore monogrammed polo shirts.

It took a month for TR's sails to arrive from Hong Kong. As soon as they had cleared customs, we headed west for the south coast of Puerto Rico. Connie flew down for a short final visit, expanding our view of the island via car rental and fine dining. Sailing from the southwest corner of Puerto Rico, our first leg west was across the Mona Passage. Although the wind was favorable, three conflicting swells gave TR an ungodly tilt and roll that had Anna turning green for the first time.

Light easterlies pushed us through the Windward Passage toward Great Inagua. Twenty miles out, a U.S. Coast Guard helicopter circled TR twice and flew off to the south. I had to wonder what the devil they were doing way down here, hundreds of miles from the American coast. Near sundown, the rakish profile of a sleek military cutter appeared above the horizon. Soon I heard them calling us on channel 16. When I replied, they said, "This is the U.S. Coast Guard, are you an American registered vessel?"

I replied to the affirmative. "Stand by, we are sending over a boarding party." Gee, I thought, welcome home. I tolerated another reaming by my own countrymen and agreed to lock the valves on TR's head when I entered U.S. waters. It really wouldn't have been so bad if they had only asked. What is so hard about that? Anna was not impressed, and she's German.

We dallied through the Bahamas, got trounced by a kick-ass northerly front, lived off nature's bounty most of the time and had a fairly soft landing easing into to the real world. We were now back to my arrival in West Palm Beach, Florida but we didn't linger, heading up the Intercoastal Waterway, aka: the Ditch, to Stuart.

We took the scenic Okeechobee Waterway across central

Florida, appreciating the alligators and bird life and kept to rural America as much as possible. From Ft. Myers we cut across the Gulf to Pensacola, our final open water passage. Our last night out Mother Nature, in her blustery best, pummeled us with booming thunder storms ripped through with lightening, horizontal rain and gusts to fifty knots. TR seemed to revel in it. I could just picture the Queen saying "Sock it to me, Mama."

I had friends in southern Alabama and that area (I'm thinking rural) seemed as good a place as any to hole up. We had no sailing plans beyond the present.

Through my friends we found Pirate's Cove, a throwback marina/boatyard from the fifties with the requisite redneck behind the bar, a classic tin roofed weathered cypress rectangle with a wrap-around porch. A few days after we'd snugged TR into a shallow muddy slip the marina population, locally known as Pirate's Cove Riff Raff, seemed to be going out of their way to accommodate us. I couldn't figure it out since we really hadn't spoken with anybody at length and we'd only said we'd come across the Gulf from Ft. Myers. Just your usual live-aboard trash. But that night at the bar, a couple of guys called me over and thrust a magazine in my face and asked, "Is this you?" It was the issue of Sail Magazine with a half page color photo of TR sailing out of Tahiti. A smidgen of notoriety goes along way towards making friends in Alabama.

For three years TR wallowed in her muddy berth, expressing her discontent by sinking herself each summer that we were gone. Winters we spent at The Cove, tending to all the Queen's ailments. I could picture Theodora with a serious pout. Anna was not allowed to leave the country while her application for permanent residence was being considered and neither of us had dreams of sailing the Gulf Coast. We decided to sell TR. A year of advertising brought nary a nibble.

Then one day my sister Carla and her husband, Ross, owners and operators of the Tinkertown Museum located in the mountains east of Albuquerque, New Mexico, called with a proposition. I listened politely in silence while my mind revolted at the very thought. TR in the museum as a nautical exhibit? This salty seagoing icon of traditional sail? I had TR's best interests at heart and felt rather offended. She had years of sailing left in her. Six months went by tick, tick, tick. No buyers, marina costs mounting, TR sunk, once again, in the mud. I called my sister back. Anna wasn't happy. She hadn't gotten cruising out of her system.

I sold TR's sails, every piece of nautical gear that wasn't bolted down and the 3 tons of lead in her bilge. When I was through she still looked like a salty old boat but she was a mere shell of herself. I couldn't look her in the eye. I told myself I was doing it for her. A nice home in the tall pines a scant thousand miles from the nearest ocean. After all, her iron fastenings were bleeding like sacrificial sheep, her oak transom was a little punky, a new engine wouldn't hurt. She paid for her own transport to Tinkertown, her last port of call, and was craned into place. Ross and I built an open shed around her with pier-like walkways extending to the rest of the museum. I knew the Queen was pissed, but didn't realize how malicious she could be until the day I was on the metal roof of the shed making slots to accommodate her rigging. I'd tied myself securely to the mast that jutted through the roof because of the steep pitch and slick surface of the painted steel. No way that knot came untied by itself. I slid off the roof, plummeting twenty feet through evergreen branches and landed with a thud on the rocky slope – Bitch! After that I was extra careful around her.

A wall size map now takes landlocked kids and international visitors on a journey around the world. A display of nautical paraphernalia gives the impression that it takes tremendous knowledge to attempt a circumnavigation. And I believe that Theodora is over her snit. I mean how could she not be with nearly everyone who passes through the museum admiring her stalwart saltiness, traditional construction and past accomplishments. What about the dreamers who stroke her bulwarks and run a fond hand along her bowsprit. And don't forget those who have nothing but loving sympathy for the poor girl who was yanked from the sea in the prime of her life and rendered useless in the godforsaken mountains awaiting the next hundred year flood. She is also a testament to my crowning achievement, which was to reverse the cash flow on a boat.

And me? Well I tried to break into the fiction market with a few adventure novels. Anna and I made a few trips back to Turkey importing <u>rugs</u>, no, scratch that, <u>kilims</u> to New Mexico. When we'd sold all the kilims we went our seperate ways. I built a few guitars on demand and tried my hand at day-trading, breaking even after five years in a volatile market. I bought a fixer-upper, actually sold it at a profit, married the woman of my dreams and now spend my winters in the Bahamas. As you might imagine the move entailed boats as well, but that, is another story.

About the Author

Fritz attended the University of New Mexico majoring in classical guitar until he woke up one morning and realized he didn't have the talent to pursue a concert career. Building guitars however, came naturally, an art he has pursued successfully since 1972. Cold weather lost its appeal after eight years of teaching skiing so he became a paramedic through the county fire department and practiced emergency medicine for seven years before setting sail. Since his return from the wet world of salt and corrosion he has penned four novels and two works of non-fiction. He met and married his wife, Mari in New Mexico, then followed a combined dream to build a home on Crooked Island in the Bahamas and resurrect a century old brick farmhouse on Washington Island, Wisconsin. He still writes and builds custom guitars.

Wait! Wait!

Reviews are a huge deal for all authors. Please take a moment and review this book on Amazon. I'd be forever grateful. (even if it's not a rave review.)

Here is the beginning of that "other story".

PLUNGE

Midlife with Snorkel

MARI ANDERSON & FRITZ DAMLER

The Bahamas

Prologue
<u>Ready, Set...</u>

Mari:

It was Monday, 5 a.m. I'd been up all night stewing about a mistake I made in an ad for a big client. An ad that right then was being distributed all over the county as part of the current year's New Mexico Vacation Guide. It was two full pages. Color. Gorgeous photos, clever copy. And the wrong toll-free number. Instead of linking callers to the right office, the phone was answered by a thick-accented man in an off-track betting lounge in New York City. He was not the least bit interested in giving up his phone number to solve my problem.

How could this have happened? So many eyes had proofread so many versions of the ad we must have become blind to the disaster that stared at us from the middle of the page. My client was understanding and gracious, but ultimately the responsibility for the goof was mine, all mine. After 24 hours of brooding I still felt like throwing up, but finally managed to nod off to sleep. That's when the phone rang.

A client who was in Boston for a conference needed to catch me, she said, before heading into all-day meetings. She was sorry to call so early, but simply had to make a change in her business brochure. A brochure that I'd delivered to the printer two days before.

As the sky started to lighten, I started the coffee maker and sifted through the previous day's mail, forcing myself to open an envelope with *Taxation and Revenue Department* as the return address. The prior year, to nudge my little business towards more financial professionalism, I'd hired a zippy new tax guy, so this shouldn't be scary. But this letter informed me my previous year's gross receipts reports didn't match the amount reported on my federal income tax. That's a big no-no. I'd not been charging tax to some clients who represented themselves as non-profit. Non-profit they may have been but without, it turns out, the requisite, official, designation. Now I'd have to go back and collect all those taxes or pay them myself, plus a hefty fine.

It was Monday, 5:30 a.m. I wasn't so tired, frustrated or stressed that I couldn't find my way through it all. But at that moment I started to wonder about my life, and about the box I'd created for myself. I started to think about how lovely but foreign the word *spacious* had begun to sound.

Fritz:

There is an old Cole Porter song that goes: *Oh give me land, lots of land, with starry skies above. Don't fence me in...* It was my theme song. After ten years at sea on a 35-foot wooden sailboat, followed by five years managing a retreat center in the mountains of New Mexico, Albuquerque's North Valley seemed pretty urban to me. Deep down I could feel the 24/7 hum of the city. I missed the quiet. I'd barricaded myself on our half acre of land. Home Depot and Barnes and Noble were within walking distance. The thought of driving across town to see a movie, eat at a restaurant, or attend a concert gave me the chills. I even found a Tae Kwon Do studio that I could get to, avoiding all but two traffic lights.

Between a bit of day trading in that crazy dot-com era and working on my third novel, I rarely had to leave the house. All my visions of paradise had those starry skies and uninterrupted vistas, be they land or sea. What would it take to change the picture? Certainly an opportunity if we recognized it as such, and of course, some money. Our finances were primarily tied up in the house, the remnants of my rug business and Mari's graphic design company. It's not like we had vast resources or big savings accounts.

But the question always remains, how thin does the ice have to get before you stop walking? Until it starts to crack? I knew I was ready to keep moving forward, and I didn't mind the thought of getting wet.

Mari/Fritz:

Talk to almost anyone, especially those of us at midlife (handy euphemism for the stage of life just prior to "old") and they will tell you of a moment, or a period of time in their lives when they could have made a radical change. And didn't. Of course, like beauty or fear, the concept of "radical change" is in the eye and emotions of the beholder. For us it might be staying home on New Year's Eve instead of going out. For you it's divorce, Peace Corps, teaching yoga in Africa.

The same goes for paradise. We say sandy beach/palm trees/salt water; you say chateau/vineyard/1-speed bicycle. (Actually, we have lots of versions of paradise and you probably do, too, depending on the season, your mood, even the day of the week.)

But even though our notions of the perfect place to be and to live may change through the years, the way to reach Nirvana never does. There's always that moment, a jumping-off point, the words, *why not?* Followed by a plunge.

This is the story of ours.

Armando's Flight

(When you see this fish it's Mari talking)

Today an elfin, curly-haired Venezuelan man dropped from the sky. A violent thunderstorm had just swept through; our aluminum shutters still pinged with the last remnants of hard, horizontal rain. The sharp smell of ozone permeated the rock walls of the house. A high-pitched buzz, distinctly different than the one small airplanes make when landing, replaced the sound of rain. Fritz looked outside just as the contraption responsible vanished beneath the line of coconut palms.

"What the devil was that?" he said. "Let's go check it out."

We quickly drove the half-mile to the landing strip. Sitting there was a tiny, torpedo-nosed bumper-car on three wheels topped with a tent pole-like framework that supported a single, triangular wing. What looked like a large lunch box covered with wires was suspended behind the seat. Attached to the lunch box, a red-tipped propeller. If Mary Poppins had decided to upgrade her umbrella, she might have gone for this machine.

It had already attracted a crowd. The pilot, who emerged smiling from the middle, looked more like Frodo the Hobbit than a prim English nanny. And like Frodo, he was on a quest.

"Armando," he said, and shook hands all around.

He'd left Orlando two days before, intending to island-hop to Caracas, Venezuela, in time for the 100-year anniversary of flight on December 17, 2004. There was going to be a big party, he told us. If he made it, his flight would earn him a mention in the Guinness Book of World Records. This meant Armando from Orlando still had over fifteen hundred miles to travel. In six days.

The original aft seat of his motorized hang-glider had been replaced by a 26-gallon fuel tank, enough for about four hours of flight. The wingspan was short by comparison to most ultra-lights; Armando's priority was speed, not glide. To make up for it he flew high. If his engine quit between 5,000 and 10,000 feet, he'd have nearly forty miles of glide time to spot an island or cay (key) for emergency landing. His little air machine had no floats; water landing was not an option.

Armando quickly began to peel off three pairs of pants, a turtleneck, two sweaters, fleece pullover and leather jacket. "It is bery, bery cold up there," he said, already sweating. It was currently 78° on the ground.

Crooked Island, Bahamas, had not been on his original itinerary but the squall with "rain like needles" forced him to descend until the storm passed. The storm was headed the same direction he was, towards the Turks and Caicos Islands. With the existing tailwind, he expected to fly at up to ninety miles per hour, easily overtaking the same conditions he'd just escaped. Already feeling deputized as ground crew in Armando's quirky campaign, Fritz and I invited him to lunch. We also offered our guest room in case he was grounded overnight.

The 1 p.m. weather report on ZNS radio predicted a cold front headed our way from the northern Bahamas. If it cleared to the south, Armando said he might chance an afternoon flight to the Turks and Caicos, or at least Mayaguana, which was a hundred miles southeast.

While we ate, we learned more about our unexpected guest. This was no boy on a coming-of-age joyride. In 1995, Armando, his wife and two children had left Venezuela for the safety of the States after two incidents. His teenaged daughter had been robbed as she left a bank in Caracas. Months later, two bullets struck his wife's car as she sped away from attempted hijackers.

Their transition was eased by Armando's dual citizenship; his father was Venezuelan, his mother American. In Orlando, he'd found work at Disney World, spending his days underwater feeding fish in the sea exhibit. He said he felt lucky to have the job. "I am scuba diver. Who could think I'd get paid to do what I love?"

By the time we finished lunch, the sky looked clear in all directions. Armando called home and left the message that he was safe and once again on his way. He also left our phone number so his wife could call us back later for details.

We drove him to the landing strip and he began to layer on all his clothing. Before the heat made him light-headed, Armando hurried through his pre-flight check while Fritz and neighbor Jim Finley released the glider's tie-down straps. Then, handshakes. Hugs. Photos and thank-you's. A promise extracted to not allow his desire for success compromise his good judgment. Another promise to call when he reached, or did not reach, his destination.

Then he pulled the crank, the engine caught, the prop whirled. He strapped himself in and taxied down the runway. When he reached the far end he pivoted, then sped past us, lifted and waved. He arced a half-circle over casuarina pines and was gone.

Fritz and I listened as the sound of the engine grew faint. The pines still radiated a shimmer of color, like the afterglow of sunset. We drove home smiling and silent.

Six days passed. We spoke of Armando every day, guessing

where he might be. From the Turks and Caicos he'd planned to stop in Puerto Plata, the Dominican Republic, then Puerto Rico and south to the Leeward, then Windward Islands: St. Croix, Saba, Nevis, St. Kitts, Montserrat, Guadeloupe, St. Lucia, St. Vincent and finally, the coast of Venezuela and home. A friend had set up a website to track his progress, but we had no way to access it.

On the evening of Wednesday the 17th, his targeted date of arrival, we decided to call his wife. Before we could dial, the phone rang. Fritz answered, and after a moment said, "Armando! Que Pasa?" Then, "At least you're safe."

He was in an airport en route to Miami, then home. As he'd left Puerto Rico his engine had begun to repeatedly stall. Even though he'd been able to restart it each time, he knew it was too dangerous to continue. True to his promise to put his safety first, he returned to Puerto Rico and caught a commercial flight home. In January he'd try again, he told Fritz, who asked him to stop again on Crooked, this time on purpose. He promised he would.

Armando's flight felt like one of those oddly wonderful events that sometimes slip through the normal matrix of time and experience. Since building a home on Crooked Island five years before, I'd almost come to expect them. Whether it was the island itself or the decision to leave urban life, career and the expectations that accompanied them, it seemed we'd put ourselves on the path of wonder.

It was inexplicable, really, why someone with a family, a home and a job would fly a machine that looked like a cereal-box prize at 10,000 feet wearing a closet-full of winter clothes. Not content with sticking a toe in, Armando had plunged into his voyage, his adventure, his dream. And so had we.

Chapter 1
A Short 5 Years

(This fish means it's Fritz talking)

How often have you returned from a vacation resolved to change your locale, your lifestyle, or at least, your priorities? Mari and I were no different. After two outrageous weeks in the far southeast Bahamas, we were drunk on sunshine, saltwater and possibility. On a moonlit beach stroll, I even popped the question: "Could you see yourself living here?"

I had the name and phone number of a Nassau real estate agent handling Crooked Island properties. But before long, the comfort and discomfort of the familiar worked like a sleeping potion to dim the dream under a blanket of routine. It would be months before I came across the scrap of paper in the deep, sawdust-filled recesses of my wallet and made the call.

It had all started innocently enough with a visit to old friends now living in the Bahamas. It was February 1997, winter in Albuquerque. Mari and I had been together a year, both of us in our high forties, both divorced. We had yet to travel anywhere of consequence together. Granted, there are worse places to spend a winter than in New Mexico, but given the choice between schussing or diving, I'll take fins and snorkel any time. And if non-stop phone calls from demanding advertising clients followed by sleepless nights were any indication, Mari was a serious candidate for some R&R. What could be better, I asked her, than spending a few weeks where it was warm, affordable and remote?

There was only one requirement: bring a cooler loaded with fresh produce and protein. The only expense beyond that, Doug and Christel assured us, would be airfare since there was no place to spend money on Crooked Island. We believed them.

Tickets were booked; house, animal and business arrangements were made. We were on our way, almost. A canceled flight collapsed our itinerary and we found ourselves on our way to Nassau, New Providence, not Georgetown, Exuma, where Doug was to meet us with his Cessna 172. I used the in-flight phone to call the only number for Crooked Island we had—Gibson's Lunchroom—and woke everyone on the plane shouting a message to stop Doug before he took off.

We spent an unplanned night in Nassau, then appeared early the next morning for the twice weekly BahamasAir flight to Crooked Island. Which was canceled and rescheduled for two hours hence. Which necessitated more phone calls, more shouting. The fact that we had a cooler full of travel-weary fruit, vegetables and meat seemed to be of no concern to the airline employees. Everyone had coolers. Everyone was getting edgy.

Two hours later an emissary from a group of restless bone-fishermen also Crooked-bound approached the desk attendant and asked when the plane would leave. This seemed reasonable, as there was nothing with wings visible in the boarding area or on the tarmac. The tall, uniformed employee checked his watch. "It will leave at eleven sir, but not exactly eleven."

He was right. At 11:20 the plane taxied into view. By 11:45 we were on our way.

Neither Mari nor I had ever seen the Bahamas from the air. We were transfixed by the surreal shades of turquoise rippled with waves of white sand that covered the Bahama Banks. I had a sense of returning home—I'd sailed through these waters several times over the past twenty years and was on intimate terms with some of its shallow sandbars.

When we left the green expanse of Long Island, the sea made an abrupt change to deep indigo as we crossed the two-mile deep Crooked Island Passage. When we deplaned, a cool ten-knot breeze and clear skies eclipsed the pains of travel. Defying the odds, Doug and Christel had received our messages and were there to greet us along with their neighbor, June McMillan, who provided the transport—a blue Toyota minivan with Capistrano painted in pink on the driver's side door.

We were initially impressed with Colonel Hill's 4000-ft. airstrip, but soon after landing began to understand why it had been difficult to unearth much information about Crooked from travel guides. Our final destination lay near the end of a twenty-mile journey over an unpaved, pitted road that for two hours brutalized the suspension system of June's minivan. No buildings rose beyond a single story. No boutiques, duty-free liquor or other strip-mall dwellers, much less a strip-mall. The nearest golf course was 250 miles behind us in Nassau.

We slalomed through Colonel Hill, the island hub of government. Its scattered Caribbean-style homes were painted in flavors of pumpkin, lime, pomegranate, lemon and persimmon. Foreign odors, from swooning sweet to earthy decay, billowed through the open windows. June, a veteran of thirty winters on Crooked Island, shared anecdotes about each settlement we passed: Cabbage Hill, Fairfield, Richmond Hill. We stopped briefly at Cripple Hill to pick up Henrietta, June's ten-year-old chicken that she and her husband Don had raised since it was hatched.

Along the way, I noticed a few bare power poles sticking out of the ground at odd angles. Christel explained that personal generators and solar panels were currently the only source of electricity, but the Bahamian government promised diesel generator-powered electricity and a paved road by the following year. Then everyone laughed.

The smile on Mari's face mirrored my own and I hoped it was for the same reason. This was definitely my kind of place. Even in our rural north Albuquerque home I felt the slow squeeze of urbanization. Here there was room to breathe and, I would discover, a place still intimate with the pulse and rhythms of the ocean; a place of deep quiet, steady winds and generous people, regularly punctuated by unusual and sometimes startling events.

Made in the USA
Columbia, SC
08 July 2021

41555375R00115